Mark 10:25: Elon Musk: Hereditary Int Machine.

Lord Leon Brittan (1939-2015): "A German Jew." Lord Denning (1899-1999).

CONTENTS:

PROLOGUE:	3
ONE:	24
TWO:	44
THREE:	73
FOUR:	92
FIVE:	107
SIX:	128
SEVEN:	139
EIGHT:	150
NINE:	162
TEN:	171
ELEVEN:	183
TWELVE:	195
ABOUT THE AUTHOR:	198

Mark 10:25: Elon Musk: Hereditary Intra-Racial Sex Machine.

PROLOGUE: Retired Senior Judge, Peter Herbert (OBE): "Racism is present in the British judicial system."

"Someone must be trusted. Let it be the Judges." Oxbridge-educated very, very, very, rich man's son (**Mark 10:25**), Lord Denning (1899-1999), unapologetic hereditary white supremacist impartial expert of their Law, a 'Pharisee' – **Luke 11:52.**

"All sections of UK society are institutionally racist." Sir, Bernard Hogan-Howe.

"Racism is rife throughout most organisations across Britain." Sir, Sadiq Khan, KBE.

Meghan Markle is impure (43% Nigerian): "Meghan Markle was the victim of explicit and obnoxious racial hatred." John Bercow, a former speaker.

Why Great Britain? There were several other Countries parasitic economic migrants could settle in.

Before Slavery, what? Gigantic yields of millions of stolen children of defenceless poor people, including the pure black African ancestors of our IMPURE DUCHESS OF SUSSEX, Princess Ada Mazi Omu of Arochukwu, Princess Meghan Markle (43% Nigerian), and her impure children (<43% Nigerian)—**Habakkuk**, not feudal agriculture, lured the Italian Jewish ancestors of Benjamin Disraeli (1804 -1881) to Great Britain. He changed his religion and blended with huge yields of several continuous centuries of MERCILESS RACIST EVIL: The greediest economic cannibalism and the evilest racist terrorism the world will ever know: They were greedier than the grave, and like death, they were never satisfied—**Habakkuk 2:5.**

The father Judges no one, but only HE has the MORAL RIGHT to appoint Judges, and the only sinless Judge was appointed by GOD—**John 5:22.**

"The only difference between the saint and the sinner is that every saint has a past, and every sinner has a future." Wilde (1854- 1900).

Only Saints have the moral right to Judge sinners—**John 8:7, Matthew 7:1–6,** as devils cannot cast out demons—**Matthew 12:27.**

'British integrity is the gold standard." Oxbridge-educated rich man's son, Lord Denning (1899–1999), paraphrased.

Brainless Racist Nonsense: Colonial Mentality. Part of the enduring residues of the original sin (SLAVERY).

"Someone must be trusted. Let it be the Judges." Oxbridge-educated rich man's son, Lord Denning (1899–1999), paraphrased

MEANING: You must trust pure white Judges.

OYINBO OLE/ODE: AN IGNORANT HEREDITARY RACIST DESCENDANT OF ULTRA-RIGHTEOUS PURE WHITE THIEVES AND OWNERS OF STOLEN CHILDREN OF DEFENCELESS POOR PEOPLE (AFRICANS) – **HABAKKUK.**

Oxbridge-educated rich man's son, Lord Denning (1899–1999): An unapologetic hereditary RACIST descendant of THIEVES, very, very, very, greedy Colonialist Economic Cannibals, Industrial-Scale Professional Drug Dealers (Opium Merchants of the Qing Dynasty), and owners of stolen children of defenceless poor people, including the pure black African ancestors of our IMPURE DUCHESS OF SUSSEX, Princess Ada Mazi Omu of Arochukwu, Princess Meghan Markle (43% Nigerian), and her impure children (<43% Nigerian)—**Habakkuk**, who was neck deep in personal and inherited sins did not have the MORAL RIGHT to Judge sinners (**John 8:7, Matthew 7:1–6**), and the dead Noble Lord shall face the sword of truth, not Jonathan Aitken's, but the Divine Sword of transparent truth—**John 5:22, Revelation 20: 11–15.**

If all the RABBIS in the Universe, including in the USA and in Israel, could disprove the TRUTH, which is that Leslie and Robert Kingston (probably arbitrarily acquired camouflage English names) are INCOMPETENT RACIST LIARS—who unrelentingly immortalised incompetent mendacity, they will confirm the belief of billions of people in our world, which is that Antichrist Islam, Antichrist Judaism, Antichrist Freemasonry Quasi-Religion (Occultist Ritualists), and all motley assemblies of exotic religions and faiths, including all the exotic religions and faiths associated with the 15 Holy Books in the House of Commons, are not intellectually flawed SATANIC MUMBO JUMBO, and they will also confirm that the fellow baselessly and brainlessly bragged about His ABSOLUTE EXCEPTIONALISM—**John 14:6.**

Ignorance is bliss: "Those who know the least obey the best." George Farquhar (1677-1707).

"Blue-eyed devils." Elijah Mohammed (1897-1975).

Matthew 12:27: Blue-eyed devils cannot cast out green-eyed demons.

"The white man was created a devil, to bring chaos upon the earth." Malcolm X (1925-1965).

Hereditary Racist Experts of English Law (New Pharisees—**Luke 10:25–37, Luke 11:52**): 'Judiciary in England and Wales 'institutionally racist', says https://www.theguardian.com › law › oct › judiciary-[i…18

Oct 2022—Exclusive: more than half of legal professionals in survey said they saw a judge acting in a racially biased way.

OYINBO OLE/ODE: If all Pure White Legal Professionals are excluded from the Guardian Survey, 50% will instantly become 100%.

<u>Stepney</u>, <u>Tower Hamlets</u> (<u>East London</u>), April 2015: "Racism is alive and well and living in Tower Hamlets, in <u>Westminster</u> and, yes, sometimes in the <u>judiciary</u>." Retired Senior Judge Peter Herbert (OBE).

"Ethnic minorities should not place their faith in a justice system that had not been designed for them" Retired Senior Judge Peter Herbert (OBE).

Based on several decades of very, very, very, proximate observations and direct experiences, homogeneity in the administration of English Law is the impregnable secure mask of MERCILESS RACIST EVIL, an intelligently designed, very, very, very, potent weapon of RACE WAR—**Habakkuk 1:4.**

Colourism, Pure Whitism and Nepotism: "Trump's administration packed courts with white Judges." KAMALA HARRIS

OYINBO OLE/ODE: Only stupid Negurs expect hereditary white supremacist Freemason Bastard Judges to measure Negurs with the same yardstick they use to measure their own pure white kindred, and only stupider Negurs expect others to voluntarily relinquish centuries-old stolen advantageous positions in exchange NOTHING.

Bernard Madoff (1938–2021) and Ján Ludvík Hyman Binyamin Hoch (1923–1991) were PROFESSIONAL PURE WHITE THIEVES—**Exodus 20:15.**

"Jews are very good with money." President Trump.

Bianca and Jared Kushner are Jews.

Judas Iscariot, Ján Ludvík Hyman Binyamin Hoch, and Bernard Madoff were Jews.

Facts are sacred: "The truth allows no choice." Dr Samuel Johnson (1709-1784).

Oxford, England: GDC, Mrs Helen Falcon, MBE, alleged Jew, and ROTARIAN (vulgarly charitable, hereditary RACIST, and Antichrist Freemasonry Quasi-Religion without voodoo or occultists' rituals) unrelentingly lied under oath and on record—**Habakkuk 1:4.** The poor pure white ancestors of her pure white father and mother were INCOMPETENT RACIST LIARS too, like the ancestors of King's School and Oxbridge-educated Lord Justice Charles Anthony Haddon-Cave, KC, a RACIST son of a very, very, very, rich TASMANIAN Colonialist Economic Cannibal (**Mark 10:25**), and an impostor and an expert of deception (perception is grander than reality), and a closeted hereditary white supremacist descendant of DRUG LORDS (opium merchants of the Qing Dynasty), and a homie of Eton and Oxbridge-educated very, very, very, rich men's son, Archbishop Justin Welby (**Mark 10:25**), they were THIEVES and owners of stolen children of defenceless poor people, including the pure black African ancestors of our IMPURE DUCHESS OF SUSSEX, Princess Ada Mazi Omu of Arochukwu, Princess Meghan Markle (43% Nigerian), and her impure children (<43% Nigerian)—**Habakkuk**.

A very, very, very, Dishonest Archetypal Pure White Englishwoman. A crooked closeted hereditary RACIST Member of the Most Excellent Order of our Empire of Stolen Inheritance—**Habakkuk 1:4.**

Mrs Helen Falcon (MBS), our hereditary RACIST pure white bastard was not deterred by his Justice—**John 5:22** because she did not believe in his exceptionalism—**John 14:6.**

BRISTOL, ENGLAND: The entire foundation of Bristol, including Bristol University where the crooked, hereditary RACIST, and homunculus pure white bastard, Mrs Helen Falcon (MBE) studied dmf (very soft shitty tooth science) was built on a foundation of BONES of stolen children of defenceless poor people, including the pure black African ancestors of our IMPURE DUCHESS OF SUSSEX, Princess Ada Mazi Omu of Arochukwu, Princess Meghan Markle (43% Nigerian), and her impure children (<43% Nigerian)—**Habakkuk**, and more BONES than the millions of skulls at the doorstep of Pol Pot (1925-1998).

GDC, Mrs Helen Falcon, MBE, alleged Jew, and a ROTARIAN (vulgarly charitable, hereditary RACIST, and Antichrist Freemasonry Quasi-Religion without voodoo or occultists' rituals): Her type killed the NIGERIAN, only 56, and the Indian, only 42, albeit remotely.

Leviticus 19:33–34: They kill foreigners just for fun, albeit hands-off, with the mens rea hidden in the belly of the actus reus.

Then, white cats used to kill black rats for food (merciless economic cannibalism), but now FAT CATS are very, very, very, bellyful, highly civilised, and super-enlightened, so they eat processed thinned foods from supermarkets, so they kill rats just for fun.

Google: Dr Richard Bamgboye, GP.

Google: Dr Anand Kamath, Dentist.

They were unlawfully killed, albeit hands-off, with the mens rea hidden in the belly of the actus reus. Only our own people (foreigners) seem to be dying in this latent., but very, very, very, potent, and raging undeclared RACE WAR. One day, a foreigner would flip and balance the unbalanced. If you chase a wild boar in the African bush, and leaves no room to escape, the hunted against the hunter (KAMIKAZE) prepared to die, but not alone, and the hunter will become the hunted.

OUR OWN NIGERIA: SHELL'S DOCILE CASH COW SINCE 1956 (OLOIBIRI). GDC WAS ESTABLISHED IN 1956.

Unlike PUTIN'S RUSSIA, there are no oil wells or gas fields in CORBY and where the pure white father and mother of Mrs Helen Falcon (MBE), Member of the Most Excellent Order of our Empire of Stolen Inheritance, were born - **Habakkuk.**

Luke 11:52: Brainless Experts of their Law: GDC, Mrs Helen Falcon, MBE, alleged Jew, and a ROTARIAN (vulgarly charitable, hereditary RACIST, and Antichrist Freemasonry Quasi-Religion without voodoo or occultists' rituals), the mind that the NIGERIAN, from shithole Africa, did not choose is FINER than your unashamedly MEDIOCRE Fish and Chips System, and he does not believe in any part of SHIT, as no part of SHIT is good, not even one – **Psalm 53**, and he has the POWER to use cogent facts and irrefutable evidence to irreparably destroy you and every part of SHIT – **Habakkuk 1:4**. Reasoning and vision do not have finite boundaries. The fellow is who He says He is – **John 14:6**. The supernatural exists and it is consistently accessible to all those who stand where it can come – **John 14:26**. You are fu*king FREE to believe whatever you like. Facts are sacred, and the right to express them should be inviolable.

"Freedom of Expression is a basic right." Lady Hale.

Bedford's District Judge Ayers: White Skin and Stolen Trust ...

https://www.amazon.co.uk › Bedfords-District-Judge-A...

Buy Bedford's District Judge Ayers: White Skin and Stolen Trust Fund. Before Slavery, What?: 100% Genetic Nigerian Whistleblowing Mole by Ekweremadu, ...

£8.19 · 30-day returns

The Law Paralysed by Michael Coleade

YouTube · SBPRA

16.9K+ views · 8 years ago

... Judge Ayers of Bedford County Court in Bedfordshire, England, could not spell the word, "emphasise" and/or did not know the meaning and ...

"Sometimes people don't want to hear the truth because they don't want their illusions destroyed." Friedrich Nietzsche (1844–1900).

BEDFORD, ENGLAND: Our own Mediocre, Wonky, Pure White Hereditary Racist, unashamedly functionally semi-illiterate, poly-educated poor man's son, a mere former debt-collector Solicitor in Norfolk/Norwich (5th Rate Partner), and the Senior Vice President of the Association of Her Majesty's District Judges, Bedford's District Judge Paul Robert Ayers, 3, St Paul's Square, MK 40 1SQ, which part of Bedfordshire Masonic Centre, MK42 8AH, and Bedford County Court, MK40 1SQ, was not STOLEN, or which part did your own pure white father and mother buy, or which part preceded SLAVERY: The Grand Buildings or their Chattels—**Exodus 20:15.**

OYINBO OLE/ODE: A STRAIGHT-FACED HEREDITARY RACIST DESCENDANT OF ULTRA-

RIGHTEOUS PURE WHITE THIEVES AND OWNERS OF STOLEN CHILDREN OF DEFENCELESS POOR PEOPLE (AFRICANS)—**HABAKKUK.**

Facts are HOLY, and repetitive Holiness are Holier. Truth is the most important attribute of the only sinless Judge who will Judge the living and the dead, including hereditary white supremacist crooked Freemason Judges – **John 5:22, Revelation 20:11-15.**

"I believe truth, the prime attribute of the Deity; and death an eternal sleep, at least of the body." Lord Byron (1788–1824).

"They tell incompetent racist lies all the time, and they lie that they don't lie." **Psalm 144.**

Psalm 116:11: "Lies are told in criminal cases. Lies are told in civil cases. Lies are told all the time." Oxbridge-educated very, very, very, rich man's son (**Mark 10:25**), Sir, Mr Justice Robert Michael Havers (1923–1992), Queen's Counsel (QC), and Attorney General.

"Truth, Sir, is the cow that would yield such people no more milk, so they are gone to milk the bull." Dr Samuel Johnson (1709–1784).

BEDFORD, ENGLAND: Our own Mediocre, Wonky, Pure White Hereditary Racist, unashamedly functionally semi-illiterate, poly-educated poor man's son, a mere former debt-collector Solicitor in Norfolk/Norwich (5th Rate Partner), and the Senior Vice President of the Association of Her Majesty's District Judges, Bedford's District Judge Paul Robert Ayers, 3, St Paul's Square, MK 40 1SQ, it is not the TRUTH that daily dialogues with PURE WHITE IMBECILES (predominantly but not exclusively pure white adults with the basic skills of a child) is a proper job that is worthwhile and manly.

"They may not have been well written from a grammatical point of view but I am confident I had not forgotten any of the facts." Crooked, Hereditary Racist, and Pure White Welsh Bastard, Geraint Evans, England's Class Welsh Postgraduate Tutor, Oxford.

SHOCKING: "Why, that is, because, dearest, you are a dunce." Dr Samuel Johnson (1709–1784).

OYINBO OLE/ODE: Our own Mediocre, Wonky, Pure White Hereditary Racist, unashamedly functionally semi-illiterate, poly-educated poor man's son, a mere former debt-collector Solicitor in Norfolk/Norwich (5th Rate Partner), and the Senior Vice President of the Association of Her Majesty's District Judges, Bedford's District Judge Paul Robert Ayers, 3, St Paul's Square, MK 40 1SQ, DISHONESTY implied that he did not know the TRUTH, which is that SLAVERY rebuilt absolutely everything it succeeded, and paid for absolutely everything it preceded, including Bedford County Court, MK40 1SQ, and Bedfordshire Masonic Centre, MK42 8AH.

OYINBO OLE/ODE: Based on cogent, irrefutable, and available evidence, prior to SLAVERY, there weren't very, very, very, many proper houses in BEDFORD.

BEDFORD, ENGLAND: GDC, Crooked, Hereditary Racist, and Pure White Bastard, Sue Gregory (OBE) unrelentingly lied under implied oath and on record— **Habakkuk 1:4.** The poor pure white ancestors of her pure white father and mother were INCOMPETENT RACIST LIARS too, like the ancestors of King's School and Oxbridge-educated Lord Justice Charles Anthony Haddon-Cave, KC, a RACIST son of a very, very, very, rich TASMANIAN Colonialist Economic Cannibal (**Mark 10:25**), a closeted hereditary white supremacist descendant of DRUG LORDS (opium merchants of the Qing Dynasty), and a homie of Eton and Oxbridge-educated very, very,

very, rich men's son, they were THIEVES and owners of stolen children of defenceless poor people, including the pure black African ancestors of our IMPURE DUCHESS OF SUSSEX, Princess Ada Mazi Omu of Arochukwu, Princess Meghan Markle (43% Nigerian), and her impure children (<43% Nigerian)—**Habakkuk.**

Had she been BLACK, or had the Judges been BLACK, she would have been in trouble – **Habakkuk 1:4.**

"Michael Jackson would have been found guilty if he'd been black." Jo Brand.

GDC, Crooked, Hereditary Racist, and Pure White Bastard, Sue Gregory (OBE): A very, very, very, dishonest typical pure white Englishwoman. A crooked closeted hereditary RACIST Officer of the Most Excellent Order of our Empire of STOLEN INHERITANCE—**Habakkuk.**

OYINBO ODE: "The English think incompetence is the same thing as sincerity." Quentin Crisp (1908-1999).

Like Hereditary White Supremacist Defenders of Faiths, and concomitantly Dissenters of the Faith – **John 14:6,** Sue Gregory (OBE) was not deterred by His Justice (**John 5:22**) because the crooked closeted white supremacist bastard, unlike HM (1926-2022) did not believe in the exclusivity and exceptionalism of the only sinless Judge – **John 14:6.**

"Jesus is the bedrock of my faith." HM (1926-2022).

They lied to their own mentally gentler white children (OECD) that they are ultra-righteous geniuses, and they don't want the pure white imbeciles they shepherd (predominantly but not exclusively pure white) to know the TRUTH, which is that apart from our INFERIOR SKIN COLOUR, and our foreign accent of speaking a foreign language, we are also properly created by Almighty God, so they criminally steal (Exodus 20:15) yields of our own people's Christ-granted talents (AFRICANS), secure in the knowledge that all Judges would be pure white and their hope is that they would be hereditary RACIST pure white bastards too – **Habakkuk 1:4.**

Our own MONEY, our own NIGERIAN children with huge oil wells and gas fields near their huts eat only 1.5/day in our own NIGERIA, very, very, very, bellyful physically ill-favoured homunculus pure white cougar, GDC, Mrs Helen Falcon, MBE, alleged Jew, and ROTARIAN (vulgarly charitable, hereditary RACIST, and Antichrist Freemasonry Quasi-Religion without voodoo or occultists' rituals), whose pure white father and mother have never seen CRUDE OIL, and whose poor pure white ancestors, including the pure white ancestors of ANEURIN BEVAN (1897–1960) and DAME MARGARET SEWARD (1935–2021), were fed like battery hens with huge yields of millions of stolen children of defenceless poor people, including the pure black African ancestors of our IMPURE DUCHESS OF SUSSEX, Princess Ada Mazi Omu of Arochukwu, Princess Meghan Markle (43% Nigerian), and her impure children (<43% Nigerian)—**Habakkuk**, was our archetypal Postgraduate Dean, Oxford, Great Britain. Which part of our own shithole AFRICA is great?

"How Europe underdeveloped Africa." Dr Walter Rodney (1942–1980).

OXFORD, ENGLAND: GDC, Crooked, Hereditary Racist, and Pure White Bastard, Mrs Helen Falcon, MBE, alleged Jew, and ROTARIAN (vulgarly charitable, hereditary RACIST, and Antichrist Freemasonry Quasi-Religion without voodoo or occultists' rituals, dishonestly implied that she did not know that SLAVERY rebuilt everything it succeeded and paid for everything it preceded, including ANEURIN BEVAN'S NHS (1948), and DAME MARGARET SEWARD'S GDC (1956).

Google: The White Judge Lied.

New Herod, **Matthew 2:16**: Deluded and conceited hereditary RACIST EVIL bastards lied to their own mentally gentler white children (OECD) and the pure white IMBECILES they shepherd (predominantly but not exclusively pure white) that they were ULTRA-RIGHTEOUS GENIUSES, and they destroy all AFRICANS who know they are not.

Matthew 2:16, Matthew 14: Ignorant RACIST BASTARDS see molecules and they destroy all NEGROES whose direct ancestors were never carried, who see QUARKS.

"The white man is the devil." Elijah Mohammed (1897-1975).

Based on several decades of very, very, very, proximate observations and direct experiences, they are Psychologically and Intellectually Insecure, and they are more impervious to other views than LUNATIC JIHADISTS, and like Trump, Xi, Putin, Kim, MBS, Babies, Etcetera, they expect everyone to love them unconditionally, and they expect the whole world to see our common world only from their own perspective, and they expect everyone to write and/or say only what they love to hear: Creeping DPRK.

They are not the only creation of Almighty God, and they are not immortal, and the universally acknowledged irrefutably SUPERIOR SKIN COLOUR that the very, very, very, fortunate wearer neither made nor chose is not the only wonder of our world.

Proverbs 20:15: Skin colour is a great creation of Almighty God, but it is not the greatest. If one's skin colour is universally acknowledged to be irrefutably superior, but if one's intellect is not, and if one is a racist crooked bastard, it is plainly deductible that Freedom of Expression is not one's best friend.

"Freedom of Expression is a basic right." Lady Hale

The ancestors of KIM did not kidnap and imprison all the people of NORTH KOREA overnight, they did gradually, and the basic right to freely disclose pictures painted by free minds was the first to be withdrawn.

"Tyrannical Police State." Elon Musk.

The second amendment was deliberately designed to guard the first: "If the Sovereign oppresses his subjects to a certain degree, they will rise and cut off his head. There is a remedy in human nature against tyranny that will keep us safe under every form of government." Dr Samuel Johnson (1709–1784).

We disagree, and our position is ABSOLUTELY IRRECONCILABLE with the position of the Defenders of Faiths, and Dissenters of our own faith, the Faith – **John 14:6**: "To disagree with three-fourths of the British public on all points is one of the first requisites of sanity, one of the deepest consolations in all moments of spiritual doubt." Wilde (1854–1900).

Several years of NAZI HOLOCAUST (1939–1945) was a mere storm in a teacup in comparison to several centuries of MAAFA (1445–1888).

Why Britain? Gigantic yields of millions of stolen children of defenceless poor people, including the pure black African ancestors of our IMPURE DUCHESS OF SUSSEX, Princess Ada Mazi Omu of Arochukwu, Princess Meghan Markle (43% Nigerian), and her impure children (<43% Nigerian)—**Habakkuk**, not feudal agriculture lured economic migrants, including Eastern European Jews, to

Great Britain. Before SLAVERY, what? Facts are sacred and cannot be overstated.

OYINBO OLE/ODE: Then, there was only subsistence feudal agriculture.

"Agriculture not only gives riches to a nation, but the only one she can call her own." Dr Samuel Johnson (1709–1784).

Exodus 20:13: Middle Passage, Mortality Rate, >20% < 100%/voyage; millions of stolen children of defenceless poor people died and became fish food in the Atlantic Ocean. Very, very, very, greedy RACIST PURE WHITE BASTARDS were not deterred by His Justice (**John 5:22**) because they did not in His exceptionalism – **John 14:6**.

"The white man is the devil." Mohammed Ali (1942–2016).

BEDFORD, ENGLAND: GDC, Crooked, Hereditary Racist, and Pure White Bastard, Freemason, Brother Richard William Hill fabricated reports and unrelentingly lied under oath and on record—**Habakkuk 1:4**. The poor pure white ancestors of his pure white father and mother were INCOMPETENT RACIST LIARS too, like the ancestors of King's School and Oxbridge-educated Lord Justice Charles Anthony Haddon-Cave, King's Counsel (KC), a RACIST son of a very, very, very, rich TASMANIAN Colonialist Economic Cannibal (**Mark 10:25**), and an impostor and an expert of deception (perception is grander than reality), and a closeted hereditary white supremacist descendant of DRUG LORDS (opium merchants of the Qing Dynasty), and a homie of Eton and Oxbridge-educated very, very, very, rich men's son, Archbishop Justin Welby (Mark 10:25), they were THIEVES and owners of stolen children of defenceless poor people, including the pure black African ancestors of our IMPURE DUCHESS OF SUSSEX, Princess Ada Mazi

Omu of Arochukwu, Princess Meghan Markle (43% Nigerian), and her impure children (<43% Nigerian)—**Habakkuk**.

Crooked, Hereditary Racist, and Pure White Bastard, Freemason, Brother Richard William Hill: A very, very, very, dishonest typical pure white Englishman. A crooked closeted hereditary RACIST FREEMASON.

"He is a typical Englishman, usually violent and always dull." Wilde (1854-1900).

"The English think incompetence is the same thing as sincerity." Quentin Crisp (1908-1999).

Whenever the true Defender of our own Faith, only our own Faith, the Faith—**John 14:6,** not President Trump, gives us the legal tools, we shall deal with the hereditary Pure White supremacist Freemason bastards (not Prince Hall Masons), and we shall use only the sword of truth, not Jonathan Aitken's, but the Divine Sword of transparent truth that is aligned to the Divine Exceptionalism of Christ (**John 14:6)**, to uncover, and irreversibly destroy the centuries-old, crooked, closeted hereditary white supremacist, vulgarly charitable, and Antichrist SATANIC MUMBO JUMBO, and we are prepared to perish in the process: Mediocre Mafia, New Pharisees **Luke 11:52**, New Good Samaritans (**Luke 10:25–37**), New Good Shepherd (**John 10:11–18**), New Truly Good God (**Mark 10:18**): Deluded, conceited, shallow and narrow half-educated school dropouts, and MF, and their superiors who wear vulgar pharisees' charitable works as cloaks of deceit, and use very, very, very, expensive colourful aprons, with vulgar embroideries, to decorate the temples of their powerless and useless fertility tools, and lie that they don't lie—**Psalm 144**, and they deceive their own mentally gentler children and the pure white imbeciles they shepherd (predominantly but not exclusively pure white) that only they and God Almighty are truly good—**Mark 10:18,** integrity, friendship, respect and charity—all for one, and one for all—**Habakkuk 1:4,** Defenders of Faiths, including all the motley assemblies of exotic faiths and religions associated with the 15 Holy Books in the House of Commons, and Dissenters of the Faith—**John 14:6**).

"Prince Charles news: Why Prince Charles would choose NOT to become Defender of the Faith. PRINCE CHARLES will become the next King of England and is currently the oldest King in Waiting in history at 71, having spent nearly his entire life as first-in-line. When he does succeed Queen Elizabeth II, however, he said he would drop one of the monarchy's core mottos. Prince Charles would become King Charles III when he succeeds his mother according to royal tradition and would take on all of the monarch's duties. While he would have to continue her work in the most part, he may also choose to make some alterations to his reign. In the past, the Duke of Cornwall has expressed his desire to change the wording of his future position. The monarch possesses a litany of titles when they accede the British throne. The Queen's full title is currently "Elizabeth the Second, by the Grace of God, of the United Kingdom of Great Britain and Northern Ireland and of Her other Realms and Territories. Queen, Head of the Commonwealth, Defender of the Faith". When Prince Charles eventually takes her position, he will inherit those titles, but he has voiced his intention to change the "Defender of the Faith" moniker. Bestowed on King Henry VIII in 1517 by the Pope, it reflects the monarch's position as supreme governor of the Church of England. Prince Charles may be known simply as "Defender of Faith". As such, it relates to their ability to preserve the national faith, which, since Henry VIII's rule is Christianity. However, in the more than 500 years since the title came into being, the UK's religious landscape has markedly diversified. The new interfaith identity of the country has led Prince Charles to voice his preference for the streamlined "Defender of Faith" instead. He revealed his intentions in 2008, in a bid to add a contemporary spin to the monarchy. British monarchs are all known as "Defender of the Faith". University College London's Constitution Unit said the move showed support for religious freedom. They said: "Charles was making the point that, in a country with many religions now present, the sovereign should be concerned to see all religion defended and not just the Church of England. "Because Latin has no definite article, he offered 'Defender of Faith' as an alternative and viable translation to signify how a sovereign should nowadays understand the contemporary meaning of the title. "In practice, religion is protected by laws made by Parliament or as a result of international agreements like the European Convention on Human Rights." Liam Doyle, 2020.

The New Pharisees, **Luke 11:52**: It is absolutely impossible for pure white supremacist Oxbridge educated rich man's son (**Mark 10:25**), Lord Justice Charles Anthony Haddon-Cave, King's Counsel (KC), KBE, and alleged 33rd Freemason (Scottish Rite), and his homie, Eton and Oxbridge-educated rich men's son, Archbishop Justin Welby (**Mark 10:25**), and all the Closeted Hereditary White Supremacist Freemason Judges in Great Britain, and all the Freemasons at the Masonic Hall, New York City, 71 W 23rd Street #1003, New York, NY 10010, United States, and all the Freemasons at Clifton Masonic Hall, 1496 Van Houten Avenue, Clifton, NJ 07013, United States, and all the Freemasons at The House of the Temple, 1733 16th Street NW Town or City Washington, D.C, United States, and all the Freemasons at the Masonic Lodge, Holly Wood Forever Cemetery, 5970 Santa Monica Boulevard, Los Angeles, CA 90038, United States, and all the 33rd Degree Freemasons at the Masonic Hall, Rising Sun, 1 Mill Road, Wellingborough NN8 1PE, and all the Freemasons at the Acacia Rooms, 27

Rockingham Road, Corby NN17 1AD, and all the Freemasons at Hotspur Lodge №1626, Fern Avenue Masonic Hall, 75–83 Fern Avenue, Jesmond, Newcastle upon Tyne NE2 2RA, and all the Freemasons at King's College School Lodge, Southside Common, London SW19 4TT, and all the members of the Bedfordshire Masonic Centre, the Keep, Bedford Road, Kempston, MK42 8AH, and all the members of Freemasons' Hall, Sheaf Close, Northampton NN5 7UL, and all the members of Towcester Masonic Centre, Northampton Road, Towcester, NN12 6LD, Northamptonshire, and all the 33rd Degree Freemasons (Scottish Rite) at Freemasons' Hall, 96 George Street, Edinburgh EH2 3DH, and all the 33rd Degree Freemasons (Scottish Rite) at the Provincial Lodge of Glasgow, 54 Berkeley Street, Glasgow G3 7DS, all the 33rd Degree Masons (Scottish Rite), at the Mother Temple, the Grand Masonic Lodge, 60 Great Queen St, London WC2B 5AZ, to disprove the truth, which is that UN Experts told the TRUTH when they corroborated Sir, Sadiq Khan, KBE, the Mayor of London's public declaration that RACIAL HATRED is rife throughout most organisations across Britain: "Africans in Great Britain are the subject of structural, institutional, and systemic racism"—UN, and they will not disprove the truth, which is that AI recklessly and incompetently lied on record (immortal mendacity), and they will not disprove the truth, which is that our Impartial Pure White Hereditary Racist Bedford's District Judge Paul Robert Ayers, >70, a Mason, and the Senior Vice President of the Association of Her Majesty's District Judges, 3, St Paul's Square, MK 401SQ, maliciously lied or he was recklessly confused (Alzheimer's disease/ Atypical Dementia) when he explicitly stated that the name of the Defendant on the approved Judgement is the name of the Defendant in the hearings before the approved Judgement, and Senior Judge, albeit England's Class, further maliciously lied or he was pathologically recklessly confused (Alzheimer's disease/Dementia), when he explicitly stated that the NIGERIAN, from shithole Africa, was invited to, and took part in, a hearing at Bedford County Court, May House, 29, Goldington Road, Bedford, MK40 3NN, on Monday, 1st July 2013, and they cannot disprove the truth, which is that Pure White Victoria Harrison, NHS Consultant, Northamptonshire PCT, unrelentingly lied under implied oath and/or record – **Habakkuk 1:4,** or she was pathologically confused (Alzheimer's disease/Atypical Dementia), and they shan't disprove the truth, which is that OXFORD, ENGLAND: NHS/GDCD/MPS/BDA, Pure White British Soldier, Territorial Defence, Stephanie Twidale (TD), unrelentingly lied under oath and on record—**Habakkuk 1:4,** and they cannot disprove the truth, which is that Pure White Kevin Atkinson, dentist, Scottish Kev, Sterling Kev, Morcott Parish Councillor, alleged Freemason, and England's Class Scottish Postgraduate Tutor, Oxford, unrelentingly LIED under oath and on record—**Habakkuk 1:4,** and they will never disprove the truth, which is that GDC/NHS, Freemason, Brother, Richard William Hill (NHS Postgraduate Tutor), fabricated reports and unrelentingly lied under oath and on record—**Habakkuk 1:4,** a very, very, dishonest white man, a closeted hereditary white supremacist NHS Postgraduate Tutor of our Empire of Stolen Inheritance—**Habakkuk,** and they will never be able to use cogent facts and irrefutable evidence to support the belief of all vulgarly charitable, Antichrist, and hereditary racist Pure White Freemasons (not Prince Hall) in the world, which is that very, very, very, vulgarly Charitable, Antichrist, and hereditary White Supremacist Freemasonry Quasi-Religion (Mediocre Mafia, New Pharisees (**Luke 11:52**), New Good Samaritans (**Luke 10: 25–37**), New Good Shepherd (**John 10: 11- 18**), New God (conceited and deluded White Supremacist bastards believe that only they and Almighty God are truly good—**Mark 10:18**), Defenders of Faiths, including all the motley assemblies of exotic faiths and religions associated with the 15 Holy Books in the House of Commons, and Dissenters of the Faith—**John 14:6)** is not an intellectually flawed SATANIC MUMBO JUMBO—centuries-old closeted hereditary white supremacists' scam, and they will not prove the belief of Dissenters of the Faith (**John 14:6)**, which is that reasoning and vision have finite boundaries. If reasoning and vision have finite boundaries, the fellow must have LIED, in the Council, before Romans and Jews, when He, purportedly, disclosed pictures His unbounded painted, and He must have also lied when He audaciously stated that He was Divinely Extraordinarily Exceptional—**John 14:6**. If the fellow told Jews and Gentiles the truth—in the Council, we are all FORKED, as His Knights attack all Kings and Queens simultaneously, and only Queens can escape, and everything that is not aligned to the exceptionalism of the Christ (**John 14:6**)—is irreversibly doomed and heading straight for the ROCKS.

"It does no harm to throw the occasional man overboard, but it does not do much good if you are steering full speed ahead for the rocks." Sir, Ian Gilmour (1926–2007), Queen's Counsel (QC), Eton and Oxford-educated rich man's son (**Mark 10:25**).

INTRA-RACIAL SEX-MACHINE, THE RICHEST MAN IN THE WORLD, IS NOT OUR GOD: **MARK 10:25.**

Proverbs 9:10, Proverbs 19:14. The INTRA-RACIAL SEX-MACHINE genius among imbeciles has unprotected sex with multiple pure white women, only pure white women, and makes loads of pure white babies he does not need, does not have time for, but can afford.

He is a GENIUS because he is the richest man in the world, a GENIUS among SPIRITUAL IMBECILES – **Matthew 19:21:**

Lord Leon Brittan (1939-2015): "A German Jew." Lord Denning (1899-1999).

ONE: "This man I thought had been a Lord among wits, but I find he is only a wit among Lords." Dr Samuel Johnson (1709–1784).

Mark 10:25: Benjamins are only about 1% of the American population, so how come 50% of billionaires in America are Benjamins?

Matthew 19:21: He ordered the RICH JEW to sell his HUGE ACQUISITIONS, give the proceeds to the poor and follow Him, he refused—**Mark 10:25.**

BEDFORD, ENGLAND: Our own Mediocre, Wonky, Pure White Hereditary Racist, unashamedly functionally semi-illiterate, poly-educated poor man's son, a mere former debt-collector Solicitor in Norfolk/Norwich (5th Rate Partner), and the Senior Vice President of the Association of Her Majesty's District Judges, Bedford's District Judge Paul Robert Ayers, 3, St Paul's Square, MK 40 1SQ, it is absolutely impossible to COMPETE on a level intellectual playing field without resorting to RACIST CRIMINALITY: No brain. Poor natural resources. Several centuries of stealing and SLAVERY preceded their HUGE STOLEN INHERITANCE—**HABAKKUK.** Before Slavery, what?

OYINBO OLE/ODE: Them, there was only subsistence feudal agriculture.

"Agriculture not only gives riches to a nation, but the only one she can call her own." Dr Samuel Johnson (1709–1784).

CORBY DENTIST, SCOTTISH KEV, KEVIN ATKINSON: BEFORE SLAVERY, WHAT?

OYINBO OLE/ODE: AN IGNORANT HEREDITARY RACIST DESCENDANT OF ULTRA-RIGHTEOUS PURE WHITE THIEVES AND OWNERS OF STOLEN

CHILDREN OF DEFENCELESS POOR PEOPLE (AFRICANS)—**HABAKKUK.**

COLOURISM/ APARTHEID BY STEALTH: SUPERIOR PURE WHITE SKIN COLOUR, A HUGE STOLEN INHERITANCE, AND WHAT ELSE? BEFORE SLAVERY, WHAT?

"Many Scots masters were considered among the most brutal, with life expectancy on their plantations averaging a mere four years. We worked them to death then simply imported more to keep the sugar and thus the money flowing. Unlike centuries of grief and murder, an apology cost nothing. So, what does Scotland have to say?" Herald Scotland: Ian Bell, Columnist, Sunday 28 April 2013

Habakkuk 2:5: They were greedier than the grave, and like death, insatiably greedy RACIST BASTARDS will never be satisfied.

The very, very, very, greedy EVIL RACIST PURE WHITE BASTARDS are no longer here, but their evil sadistic genes continue to flow through the veins of their direct descendants who remain here.

We are all who we are, the inheritors of our inheritances, genes of our individual ancestors.

OYINBO OLE: AN IGNORANT HEREDITARY RACIST DESCENDANT OF THIEVES—**HABAKKUK.**

His type killed the NIGERIAN, only 56, and the INDIAN, only 42, albeit hands-off, with the mens rea hidden in the belly of the actus reus.

Google: Dr Richard Bamgboye, GP.

Google: Dr Anand Kamath, Dentist.

Facts are sacred and they cannot be overstated.

The EVIL RACIST BASTARDS should stay here, it is safer, for, there, we shall take revenge—**Exodus 21:23–27,** but only with the sword of unrestricted truths.

CONFLICT OF INTEREST: They use Harassment Laws to stifle the disclosure of their racist criminality: "There is not a truth existing which I fear... or would wish unknown to the whole world." President Thomas Jefferson (1743-1826).

"We shall deal with the racist bastards when we get out of prison," Comrade Robert Mugabe (1924 – 2019).

Revelation 20: 11–15: Evil RACIST pure white bastards will face the sword of truth, not Jonathan Aitken's, but the DIVINE SWORD OF TRANSPARENT TRUTH – **John 5:22.**

Wales, GDP, <£90 billion, a mere Quasi-Province of London, GDP, Greater London, >£500 billion: GDC, Crooked, Hereditary RACIST, and pure white Welsh bastard, Geraint Evans, England's Class Welsh Senior Postgraduate Tutor, Oxford, unrelentingly lied under implied oath and on record—**Habakkuk 1:4.** The poor pure white ancestors of his pure white father and mother were incompetent RACIST LIARS too, like the ancestors of King's School and Oxbridge-educated Lord Justice Charles Anthony Haddon-Cave, KC, a RACIST son of a very, very, very, rich TASMANIAN Colonialist Economic Cannibal (**Mark 10:25**), and an impostor and an expert of deception (perception is grander than reality), and a closeted white supremacist descendant of DRUG LORDS (opium merchants of the Qing Dynasty), and a homie of Eton and Oxbridge-educated rich men's son, Archbishop Justine Welby (**Mark 10:25**), they were THIEVES (**Exodus 20:15**), Racist Murderers (**Exodus 20:13**), and owners of stolen children of defenceless poor people, including the pure black African ancestors of our IMPURE DUCHESS

OF SUSSEX, Princess Ada Mazi Omu of Arochukwu, Princess Meghan Markle (43% Nigerian), and her impure children (<43% Nigerian)—**Habakkuk**.

A very, very, very, DISHONEST typical pure white Welshman. A Crooked Closeted Hereditary Racist Senior Postgraduate Tutor, Oxford, albeit England's Class.

Google: Mediocre Great England.

Letters of a Racist Crooked Imbecile Welsh Dentist, Geraint ...

https://www.amazon.co.uk › Letters-Crooked-Imbecile-...

Geraint. R. Evans—BDS (Bham), MSc GDP, Cert Clin Ed, Cert Implant: Letters and Lies of a Crooked Racist Welsh Imbecile. Google: Mediocre GDC.

£10.44

BEDFORD, ENGLAND: Our own Mediocre, Wonky, Pure White Hereditary Racist, unashamedly functionally semi-illiterate, poly-educated poor man's son, a mere former debt-collector Solicitor in Norfolk/Norwich (5th Rate Partner), and the Senior Vice President of the Association of Her Majesty's District Judges, Bedford's District Judge Paul Robert Ayers, 3, St Paul's Square, MK 40 1SQ, the mind that the NIGERIAN, from shithole AFRICA, did not choose is FINER than your unashamedly MEDIOCRE Fish and Chips Justice System, and he does not believe in any part of SHIT, as no part of SHIT is good, not even one—**Psalm 53,** and he has the POWER to use cogent facts and irrefutable evidence to irreparably destroy you and every part of SHIT—**Habakkuk 1:4.** Facts are sacred and cannot be overstated.

Habakkuk 1:4: Crooked hereditary RACIST pure white bastards (predominantly but not exclusively pure white):

Then, they won in crooked courts before crooked Judges, but in the WAR when the Corporal flipped, the only sinless Judge looked away (**John 5:22**), and insatiably greedy RACIST bastards lost everything and more.

OXFORD, ENGLAND: GDC, Crooked, Hereditary Racist Pure White British Soldier (Territorial Defence), Stephanie Twidale (TD), ugly alleged Jew, uglier than Edwina Currie, unrelentingly lied under oath and on record—**Habakkuk 1:4.** The poor pure white ancestors of her pure white father and mother were incompetent RACIST LIARS too, like the ancestors of King's School and Oxbridge-educated Lord Justice Charles Anthony Haddon-Cave, KC, a RACIST son of a very, very, very, rich TASMANIAN Colonialist Economic Cannibal (**Mark 10:25**), and an impostor and an expert of deception (perception is grander than reality), and a descendant of DRUG LORDS (opium merchants of the Qing Dynasty), and a homie of Eton and Oxbridge-educated rich men's son, Archbishop Justine Welby (**Mark 10:25**), they were THIEVES (**Exodus 20:15**), Racist Murderers (**Exodus 20:13**), and owners of stolen children of defenceless poor people, including the pure black African ancestors of our IMPURE DUCHESS OF SUSSEX, Princess Ada Mazi Omu of Arochukwu, Princess Meghan Markle (43% Nigerian), and her impure children (<43% Nigerian)—**Habakkuk.**

"Could you take on the RUSSIANS by yourselves." President Trump

The YANKS are NATO, and absolutely everything else is an auxiliary bluff.

John 14:26: When the DIVINE HELPER unravels hereditary MERCILESS RACIST HATRED, to save face, members of their brainlessly and baselessly self-awarded SUPERIOR RACE unleash their Evil Racist Thunder: The Lunatic Negro Card. Any NEGRO who disagrees with any member of their brainlessly and baselessly self-awarded SUPERIOR RACE - is MENTAL: Colonial Mentality, part of the enduring residues of the Original Sin (SLAVERY).

"He has refused to submit to a medical examination." King's School and Oxbridge-educated Lord Justice Charles Anthony Haddon-Cave, King's Counsel (KC), a RACIST son of a very, very, very, RICH Tasmanian Colonialist Economic Cannibal (**Mark 10:25**), and a descendant of DRUG LORDS (opium merchants of the Qing Dynasty).

OYINBO OLE/ODE: AN ULTRA-RIGHTEOUS DESCENDANT OF PURE WHITE THIEVES AND OWNERS OF STOLEN CHILDREN OF DEFENCELESS POOR PEOPLE (AFRICANS)—**HABAKKUK.**

Industrial-Scale Professional DRUG LORDS: Evil Opium Merchants of the Qing Dynasty exported > 7000 tons/Annum. Millions succumbed to evil addiction

Properly rehearsed ultra-righteousness and deceptively schooled civilised decorum were preceded by several centuries of MERCILESS RACIST EVIL: Several continuous centuries of the greediest economic cannibalism and the evilest racist terrorism the world will ever know— **Habakkuk.**

"England is like a prostitute who, having sold her body all her life, decides to close her business, and then tells everybody she wants to be chaste and protect her flesh as if it were jade." He Manzi (1919–2009).

37, Wimpole Street, London, W1G 8DQ: Crooked, Hereditary RACIST, and pure white bastard, GDC Manager, Jonathan Martin, poly-educated pure white rubbish (not Russell Group Inferior Class Alternative Education— **Proverbs 17:16**) unrelentingly lied under oath and/or on record—**Habakkuk 1:4.**

Racist Lies and Letters, 2011: Jonathan Martin GDC …

Amazon UK

https://www.amazon.co.uk › Racist-Lies-Letters-2011-I…

Buy Racist Lies and Letters, 2011: Jonathan Martin GDC Manager, 37, Wimpole Street, London, W1G 8DQ: Antichrist, Mediocre, and Institutionally Racist.

£10.00

New Herod, **Matthew 2:16:** They lied to their mentally gentler white children (OECD) and the pure white IMBECILES they shepherd (predominantly but not exclusively pure white) that they are ULTRA-RIGHTEOUS GENIUSES, and they destroy those who know that they are not.

"The best opportunity of developing academically and emotional." Our own Mediocre, Wonky, Pure White Hereditary Racist, unashamedly functionally semi-illiterate, poly-educated poor man's son, a mere former debt-collector Solicitor in Norfolk/Norwich (5th Rate Partner), and the Senior Vice President of the Association of Her Majesty's District Judges, Bedford's District Judge Paul Robert Ayers, 3, St Paul's Square, MK 40 1SQ.

BRAINLESS RACIST NONSENSE.

"I don't want to talk grammar. I want to talk like a lady." George Bernard Shaw (1856-1950)..

"Yes, Sir, it does her honour, but it would do nobody else honour. I have indeed not read it all. But when I take up the end of a web, and find a packthread, I do not expect, by looking further, to find embroidery." Dr Samuel Johnson (1709-1784).

Our own Mediocre, Wonky, Pure White Hereditary Racist, unashamedly functionally semi-illiterate, poly-educated poor man's son, a mere former debt-collector Solicitor in Norfolk/Norwich (5th Rate Partner), and the Senior Vice President of the Association of Her Majesty's District Judges, Bedford's District Judge Paul Robert Ayers, 3, St Paul's Square, MK 40 1SQ, a brainless hereditary RACIST pure white bastard approved and immortalised what his own pure white mother and father spoke, the type of STORIES his pure white mother and father used to tell when they returned home from their regular pub crawl: Queen Victoria, Nag's Head, Greene King Etcetera, at very, very, very, odd hours, thoroughly stoned, hungry, angry, and very, very, very, RANDY, and which his pure white poly-educated supervisors and superiors in LUTON authorised – **Habakkuk 1:4.**

OYINBO OLE/ODE: Based on cogent, irrefutable, and available evidence, those who nearly passed or just passed the A/Level could do Law within one of the dullest adult populations in the industrialised world (OECD).

"Find the truth and tell it." Harold Pinter (1930-2008).

HHJ Perusko studied law at poly: Not Russell Group Inferior Class Alternative Education—**Proverbs 17:16.**

Google: HHJ Perusko studied law at poly.

"To survive, you must tell stories." Umberto Eco (1932–2016)

Just as it was in Professor Stephen Hawking's School, then, at the University of Lagos, the brightest students did mathematics, physics, and chemistry, and did not attend lectures at the Faculty of Law.

"In my school, the brightest boys did math and physics, the less bright did physics and chemistry, and the least bright did biology. I wanted to do math and physics, but my father made me do chemistry because he thought there would be no jobs for mathematicians." Dr Stephen Hawking (1942–2018).

New Pharisees, Experts of their Law, **Luke 11:52**: Their grossly overrated, overhyped, overpopulated, and mediocre trade that is dying slowly and imperceptibly, and is overseen by the Antichrist Racist Freemasons (Mediocre Mafia)— **Habakkuk 1:4; John 8:44; John 10:10.**

"The legal system lies at the heart of any society, protecting rights, imposing duties, and establishing a framework for the conduct of almost every social, political, and economic activity. Some argue that the law is in its death throes while others postulate a contrary prognosis that discerns numerous signs of law's enduring strength. Which is it?" Professor Raymond Wacks, Emeritus Professor of Law, Hong Kong

Facts are sacred.

BEDFORD, ENGLAND: Our own Mediocre, Wonky, Pure White Hereditary Racist, unashamedly functionally semi-illiterate, poly-educated poor man's son, a mere former debt-collector Solicitor in Norfolk/Norwich (5th Rate Partner), and the Senior Vice President of the Association of Her Majesty's District Judges, Bedford's District Judge Paul Robert Ayers, 3, St Paul's Square, MK 40 1SQ, a brainless hereditary RACIST pure white bastard was granted the platform to display hereditary prejudice: The land on which he was born yields only FOOD, he is semi-illiterate, and he is RICH, and he DISHONESTLY implied that he did not know that the poor pure white ancestors of his pure white father and mother were THIEVES and owners of stolen children of defenceless poor people, including the pure black African ancestors of our IMPURE DUCHESS OF SUSSEX, Princess Ada Mazi Omu of Arochukwu, Princess Meghan Markle (43% Nigerian), and her impure children (<43%

Nigerian)—**Habakkuk**, and he also DISHONESTLY implied that he did not know that SLAVERY rebuilt everything it succeeded and paid for everything it preceded, including Bedford County Court, MK 40 1SQ, and Bedfordshire Masonic Centre MK42 8DQ, and he further lied when he DISHONESTLY implied that he did not know that equitable, fair, and just REPARATION pends, and several centuries of unpaid interest accrue.

OYINBO OLE/ODE: A RACIST DESCENDANT OF THIEVES – **HABAKKUK**.

If the opportunist RACIST pure white bastard read his approved Judgement, he was a FOOL, and if he did not, he lied as he implied that he did—**Habakkuk 1:4**. The poor pure white ancestors of the pure white father and mother of the poly-educated (not Russell Group Inferior Class Alternative Education—**Proverbs 17:16**) hereditary RACIST pure white bastard were incompetent RACIST LIARS too, like the ancestors of King's School and Oxbridge-educated Lord Justice Charles Anthony Haddon-Cave, KC, a RACIST son of a very, very, very, rich TASMANIAN Colonialist Economic Cannibal (**Mark 10:25**), and an impostor and an expert of deception (perception is grander than reality), and a closeted white supremacist descendant of DRUG LORDS (opium merchants of the Qing Dynasty), and a homie of Eton and Oxbridge-educated rich men's son, Archbishop Justine Welby (**Mark 10:25**), were THIEVES (**Exodus 20:15**), Racist Murderers (**Exodus 20:13**), and owners of stolen children of defenceless poor people, including the pure BLACK AFRICAN ancestors of the IMPURE (<43% Nigerian) great grandchildren of the Duke of Edinburgh of Blessed Memory (1921–2021).

Google: Opium War (1839–1842).

Google: Opium trade (1844–1912).

John 14:6: "Jesus is the bedrock of my faith." HM (1926–2022). **Philippians 1:21**: Phillip was a 33rd Degree Freemason (Scottish Rite).

Based on several decades of very, very, very, proximate observations and direct experiences, they hate us, and we know. They hate our children more, but they don't know. No brain. Poor natural resources. Several continuous centuries of stealing and SLAVERY preceded their huge stolen inheritance – **Habakkuk**.

They don't want their own mentally gentler WHITE CHILDREN (OECD) and the pure white imbeciles they shepherd (predominantly but not exclusively pure white) to know the TRUTH, which is that apart from our inferior darker coat, which we neither made nor chose, and our foreign accent of speaking their language (a foreign language), our own people (BLACKS), are also properly created by Almighty God, and to conceal these TRUTHS, hereditary RACIST pure white bastards (predominantly but not exclusively pure white) criminally STEAL (Exodus 20:15) yields of our people's Christ-granted talents, and secure in the knowledge that all Judges would be pure white, and their hope is that they would be hereditary white supremacist bastards too—**Habakkuk 1:4.**

OYINBO OLE: OUR OWN NIGERIA, SHELL'S DOCILE CASH COW SINCE 1956 (OLOIBIRI). GDC WAS ESTABLISHED IN 1956—**HABAKKUK.**

Unlike PUTIN'S RUSSIA, there are no oil wells or gas fields in bland and colourless NORFOLK/NORWICH (Coastal Dole/the Departure Lounge of Life) and where the pure white father and mother of our own Mediocre, Wonky, Pure White Hereditary Racist, unashamedly functionally semi-illiterate, poly-educated poor man's son, a mere former debt-collector Solicitor in Norfolk/Norwich (5th Rate Partner), and the Senior Vice President of the Association of

Her Majesty's District Judges, Bedford's District Judge Paul Robert Ayers, 3, St Paul's Square, MK 40 1SQ, were born.

"Who am I to Judge?" Pope Francis (1936–2025).

The Father Judges no one (**John 5:22**).

John 8:7, Matthew 7:1–6: A brainless hereditary RACIST PURE WHITE BASTARD was granted the platform to display hereditary prejudice, and the opportunist RACIST pure white bastard ultra-righteously sat on the BONES of stolen children of defenceless poor people, including the pure black African ancestors of our IMPURE DUCHESS OF SUSSEX, Princess Ada Mazi Omu of Arochukwu, Princess Meghan Markle (43% Nigerian), and her impure children (<43% Nigerian)—**Habakkuk**, more BONES than the millions of skulls at the doorstep of POL POT (1925–1998), and the thoroughly deluded and conceited SELF-AWARDED New Christ (**John 5:22**) Judged SINNERS – **Matthew 7:1-6, John 8:7**.

OYINBO OLE/ODE: A SCATTER-HEAD HEREDITARY RACIST PURE WHITE BASTARD—**HABAKKUK**. PERCEPTION IS GRANDER THAN REALITY. SUPERIOR PURE WHITE SKIN, A HUGE STOLEN INHERITANCE, AND WHAT ELSE?

Bedford's District Judge Ayers: White Skin and Stolen Trust ...

https://www.amazon.co.uk › Bedfords-District-Judge-A...

Buy Bedford's District Judge Ayers: White Skin and Stolen Trust Fund. Before Slavery, What?: 100% Genetic Nigerian Whistleblowing Mole by Ekweremadu, ...
£8.19 · 30-day returns

Facts are sacred and cannot be overstated.

BEDFORD, ENGLAND: Our own Mediocre, Wonky, Pure White Hereditary Racist, unashamedly functionally semi-illiterate, poly-educated poor man's son, a mere former debt-collector Solicitor in Norfolk/Norwich (5th Rate Partner), and the Senior Vice President of the Association of Her Majesty's District Judges, Bedford's District Judge Paul Robert Ayers, 3, St Paul's Square, MK 40 1SQ, one-dimensionally educated shallow RACIST BASTARD, only his universally acknowledged irrefutable superior skin colour and GOD are truly good—**Mark 10:18**, and he neither made nor chose it, and he would be considerably diminished as a human being without it, and the opportunist RACIST BASTARD knows it. Based on very, very, very, proximate observations and direct experiences, the crooked hereditary RACIST pure white Judge looked like someone from a very, very, very, poor family.

FLAT TRACK BULLIES: GOOGLE: IMAGBON, 1892.

"Ethical Foreign Policy." Robin Cook (1946–2005).

Their hairs stand on end when challenged by AFRICANS, we and our type are the ones hereditary RACIST BASTARDS would beat up without the support of the YANKS.

Trump's Poodles: If BUILDERS, occultist ritualist bastards are as brave as they BRAG, they must use extreme overwhelming violence to evict PUTIN from Crimea, he used extreme overwhelming violence to convert Bakhmut from bricks to rubble and stole it—**Exodus 20:15.**

SLAVERY immeasurably transformed the standard of living of thoroughly wretched Barbarians, mere rabbit hunters, and agricultural labourers (SERFS) who lived off the land, but the intellects of their direct descendants seem untouched.

1976–2022: Our own Mediocre, Wonky, Pure White Hereditary Racist, unashamedly functionally semi-illiterate, poly-educated poor man's son, a mere former debt-collector Solicitor in Norfolk/Norwich (5th Rate Partner), and the Senior Vice President of the Association of Her Majesty's District Judges, Bedford's District Judge Paul Robert Ayers, 3, St Paul's Square, MK 40 1SQ, a brainless hereditary RACIST pure white bastard sat on a highchair that his own pure white father and mother could not afford, and which the pure white IMBECILES who sat before him (predominantly but not exclusively pure white) could not, and did not buy, in a very, very, very, GRAND COURT that was preceded by SLAVERY, future flats and absolutely inevitably distant futures NUCLEAR ASH.

29, Goldington Road, Mk40 3NN, is a block of flats.

Exodus 21:23-27: He should fu*king stay here, it is safer, and Sir Keir Starmer, a mere Trump's Poodle does not have the power over anything in the AFRICAN BUSH, and if he comes there without a lot of armed security guards, extremely nasty people would sell him just as his ancestors sold theirs. Dr Mungo Park (1771-1806) had guns. Then, he was killed, but now, he would be sold.

SLAVERY IS IMMORTAL: SUBSTITUTION IS FRAUDULENT EMANCIPATION – **HABAKKUK.**

Only our visible chains are off, our true chains will never be voluntarily removed. No people will voluntarily relinquish several centuries-old advantageous positions in exchange for NOTHING, substitution is likely.

"How Europe underdeveloped Africa." Dr Walter Rodney (1942–1980).

Equitable, fair, and just reparation pends, and several continuous centuries of unpaid interest accrue - **Habakkuk.**

OYINBO OLE: Then, they carried and sold millions of stolen children of defenceless poor people, including the pure BLACK AFRICAN ancestors of the IMPURE (<43% Nigerian), now GREEDY RACIST THIEVES steal our own natural resources from our own AFRICA—**Exodus 20:15.**

"Moderation is a virtue only among those who are thought to have found alternatives." Dr Henry Kissinger (1923–2023).

NIGER'S URANIUM: American and Russian Soldiers amicably camped side by side near NIGER'S URANIUM.

Nigerien babies with huge URANIUM MINES near their huts eat only 1.5/day in our own WEST AFRICA, a very, very, very, bellyful pure white bastard, a mere poly-educated former debt-collector Solicitor in bland and colourless NORWICH (5th Rate Partner), was granted to platform to display hereditary prejudice, and the opportunist RACIST pure white bastard thrives in GREAT BRITAIN. Which part of SHIT is great?

They are crooked, hereditary RACIST, and pure white EVIL BASTARDS, and they get away with MERCILESS RACIST EVIL because they Judge everyone, including themselves. **John 5:22**: God Almighty Judges no one.

BEDFORD,ENGLAND: GDC, Crooked, Hereditary RACIST, and pure white Freemason, Brother Richard William Hill fabricated reports and unrelentingly lied under oath and on record—**Habakkuk 1:4**. The poor pure white ancestors of his pure white mother and father were in competent RACIST LIARS too, like the ancestors of King's School and Oxbridge-educated Lord Justice Charles Anthony Haddon-Cave, KC, a RACIST son of a very, very,

very, rich TASMANIAN Colonialist Economic Cannibal (**Mark 10:25**), and a descendant of DRUG LORDS (opium merchants of the Qing Dynasty), and a homie of Eton and Oxbridge-educated rich men's son, Archbishop Justine Welby (**Mark 10:25**), were THIEVES (**Exodus 20:15**), Racist Murderers (**Exodus 20:13**), and owners of stolen children of defenceless poor people, including the pure black African ancestors of our IMPURE DUCHESS OF SUSSEX, Princess Ada Mazi Omu of Arochukwu, Princess Meghan Markle (43% Nigerian), and her impure children (<43% Nigerian)—**Habakkuk**.

A very, very, very, DISHONEST typical pure white Englishman. A crooked closeted hereditary RACIST Freemason.

Racist Lies of Crooked Kevin Atkinson, Scottish Kev, Corby ...

https://www.amazon.com › Crooked-Atkinson-Scottish-...

Buy Racist Lies of Crooked Kevin Atkinson, Scottish Kev, Corby Dentist, Alleged Freemason, and Councillor Morcott Parish.: Ugly Dalit, Suella Braverman, ...

US$7.99

They don't want their own mentally gentler white children (OECD) and the pure white IMBECILES they shepherd (predominantly but not exclusively pure white) to know the TRUTH, which is that apart from our INFERIOR SKIN COLOUR, which we neither made nor chose, and our foreign accent of speaking a foreign language, we are also properly created by Almighty God, and to conceal this TRUTH, and to save face, hereditary RACIST pure white bastards (predominantly but not exclusively pure white) criminally steal yields of our own people's Christ-granted talents (NEGROES), secure in the knowledge that all Judges would be PURE WHITE (Archie is impure, <43% Nigerian), and their hope is that they would all be hereditary white supremacist bastards too – **Habakkuk 1:4.**

Scotland, GDP, < £230 billion, a mere Quasi-Province of London, GDP, Greater London, >£500 billion: GDC, Crooked, Hereditary Racist, and Pure White Scottish Bastard, Sterling Kev, England's Class Senior Scottish Postgrad Tutor, Oxford, unrelentingly lied under oath and on record – **Habakkuk 1:4.** The poor pure white ancestors of his pure white father and mother were incompetent RACIST LIARS too, like the ancestors of King's School and Oxbridge-educated Lord Justice Charles Anthony Haddon-Cave, KC, a RACIST son of a very, very, very, rich TASMANIAN Colonialist Economic Cannibal (**Mark 10:25**), and a descendant of DRUG LORDS (opium merchants of the Qing Dynasty), and a homie of Eton and Oxbridge-educated rich men's son, Archbishop Justine Welby (**Mark 10:25**), they were THIEVES (**Exodus 20:15**), Racist Murderers (**Exodus 20:13**), and owners of stolen children of defenceless poor people, including the pure black African ancestors of our IMPURE DUCHESS OF SUSSEX, Princess Ada Mazi Omu of Arochukwu, Princess Meghan Markle (43% Nigerian), and her impure children (<43% Nigerian)—**Habakkuk.**

A very, very, very, dishonest typical pure white Scotchman. A crooked closeted hereditary racist England's Class Scottish Senior Postgraduate Tutor, Oxford, with ZERO tangible Postgraduate Qualification, not even one.

OUR OWN NIGERIA: SHELL'S DOCILE CASH COW SINCE 1956 (OLOIBIRI). GDC WAS ESTABLISHED IN 1956.

Unlike PUTIN'S RUSSIA, there are no gas fields in GLASGOW and where the pure white father and mother of

Kevin Atkinson were born. There is oil in the North Sea, but it is not a Sea of oil.

OYINBO OLE/ODE: AN IGNORANT HEREDITARY RACIST DESCENDANT OF ULTRA-RIGHTEOUS PURE WHITE THIEVES AND OWNERS OF STOLEN CHILDREN OF DEFENCELESS POOR PEOPLE (AFRICANS) – **HABAKKUK.**

Our own NIGERIAN BABIES with huge oil wells and gas fields near their huts eat only 1.5/day in our own NIGERIA, very, very, very, bellyful Kevin Atkinson, a crooked, hereditary RACIST, and pure white Scottish Bastard, a mere Corby Dentist whose pure white mother and father have never seen CRUDE OIL or gas field, and whose pure white ancestors, including John Foster (1759–1832) of BEDFORD, Robert Hibbert (1769–1849) of LUTON, and Richard Oswald (1705-1784) of GLASGOW, were fed like battery hens with yields of millions of stolen children of defenceless poor people, including the pure black African ancestors of our IMPURE DUCHESS OF SUSSEX, Princess Ada Mazi Omu of Arochukwu, Princess Meghan Markle (43% Nigerian), and her impure children (<43% Nigerian)—**Habakkuk,** thrives in Great Britain. Which part of our own shithole AFRICA is great?

Maxwell, the Aristocratic Scottish name, was not the real name of Ghislaine Maxwell's dad, it was Ján Ludvík Hyman Binyamin Hoch (1923–1991), and the JEW came from Czechoslovakia in the 40s.

Kevin Atkinson, Corby Dentist, what's the real name of your own father, where did he come from, and when?

Kevin Atkinson, Corby Dentist, when did your father acquire a camouflage Scottish name, or did your ancestors evolve from MAMI WATA in the River Ness in Inverness?

Rifkind is not a Lithuanian name, the ancestors Sir, Malcom Rifkind, came to Great Britain – from Lithuania in the 1890s. Gigantic yields of millions of stolen children of defenceless poor AFRICANS, not feudal agriculture, lured Eastern European Jews to Great Britain. Before Slavery, what?

"Those who know the least obey the best." George Farquhar (1677-1707).

A BRAINLESS HEREDITARY RACIST PURE WHITE SCOTTISH BASTARD: PERCEPTION IS GRANDER THAN REALITY. EVERYTHING, ABSOLUTELY EVERYTHING, IS BASELESSLY AND BRAINLESSLY ASSUMED IN FAVOUR OF THE UNIVERSALLY ACKNOWLEDGED IRREFUTABLY SUPERIOR SKIN COLOUR THAT THE VERY, VERY, VERY, FORTUNATE WEARER NEITHER MADE NOR CHOSE.

OYINBO OLE/ODE: AN IGNORANT DESCENDANT OF THIEVES (**EXODUS 20:15**) AND OWNERS OF STOLEN CHILDREN OF DEFENCELESS POOR PEOPLE (AFRICANS)—**HABAKKUK.**

Saxe-Coburg, and Gotha, family acquired a camouflage English name in 1917.

Gustav Liebson (1876–1947) acquired a camouflage English name in 1925, had he not, Nigel Lawson (1932–2023) would not have been our Chancellor.

Michael Portillo, Mohammed Al Fayed (1929–2023), and Ali Kemal (1867–1922) did not arbitrarily acquire camouflage English names.

Had Ali Kemal been as rich as Mohammed Al Fayed, Boris Johnson would be Mohammed Ali, and he wouldn't have been our Premier.

Kevin Atkinson, your Scottish ancestors were Racist Murderers (**Exodus 20:13**), THIEVES (**Exodus 20:15**), and owners of stolen children of defenceless poor people, including the pure black African ancestors of our IMPURE DUCHESS OF SUSSEX, Princess Ada Mazi Omu of Arochukwu, Princess Meghan Markle (43% Nigerian), and her impure children (<43% Nigerian)—**Habakkuk**.

"The supreme vice is shallowness." Wilde (1854–1900).

Mark 10:25: The richest man in the world, a mere GENIUS among imbeciles, is so shallow and narrow, he is oblivious to the notion of relativity, and can't perceive infinite reasoning and vision, and can't discern the SUPERNATURAL, which is consistently accessible to those who stand where it can come—**John 14:26**.

"We build too many walls and not enough bridges." –Sir Isaac Newton (1643–1727), devout, albeit an unorthodox Christian

"We have decommissioned natural selection and must now look deep within ourselves and decide what we wish to become." –Dr Edward. O. Wilson (1929–2021).

Satanic networks (New Pharisees) seem to think that they are our new truly good new God—**Mark 10:18.**

"The supreme vice is shallowness." Wilde (1854–1900).

RACIST ANTICHRIST BUILDERS: Deluded decorticate fools brainlessly and baselessly self-awarded the monopoly of knowledge; scatter-head shepherds of unnatural extinction. Sheep unnatural shepherd sheep. Shepherds know that sheep are morons, but sheep do not know that shepherds are morons too.

"Mediocrity weighing mediocrity in the balance, and incompetence accompanying its brother.........." Wilde (1854–1900)

Mark 10:25: Elon Musk: Hereditary Intra-Racial Sex Machine.

TWO: The supreme power that Dr Stephen Hawking (1942–2018) implied is behind the glories of the universe, must have preceded it, and must have infinite vision, and reasoning power.

"You cannot understand the glories of the universe without believing there is some Supreme Power behind it." Dr Stephen Hawking (1942–2018), an atheist science genius who believed in supernatural supreme power

"That deep emotional conviction of the presence of a superior reasoning power, which is revealed in the incomprehensible universe, forms my idea of God." –Albert Einstein (1879–1955), a Quasi-Atheist Geniuses who believed in supernatural supreme power.

"Jesus is the bedrock of my faith." HM (1926–2022).

Based on cogent, irrefutable, and available evidence, they are very, very, very, hardened PURE WHITE RACIST CRIMINALS (predominantly but not exclusively pure white), including their Judges, but not all—**Habakkuk 1:4.**

Based on cogent, irrefutable, and available evidence, the administration of English Law is an intelligently designed weapon of RACE WAR—**Habakkuk 1:4.**

Homogeneity in the administration of British Law is an impregnable secure mask of merciless RACIST EVIL.

SLAVERY IS IMMORTAL: Only our visible chains are off, our true chains will never be voluntarily removed.

"How Europe underdeveloped Africa." Dr Walter Rodney (1942–1980).

We are powerless, and we have been robbed to penniless since their armed ancestors (armed hunters of unarmed men)

found our ancestors in the AFRICAN BUSH in the 15th century: Edumare gba wa o! Only Christ has the POWER to free our people from the clamped Jaws of the crocodile, and He will whenever He wants.

Based on several decades of very, very, very, proximate observations and direct experiences, they are ANTICHRIST EVIL RACIST CRIMINALS, and they know that they are, and when they know you do too, you have reached the end of your life—a dead man walking—as all loose ends must be tied by every means necessary.

Their people are everywhere, and they control almost everything, including RACIAL HATRED and FRAUD: Integrity, friendship, respect, and charity—all for one, and one for all.

John 14:26: When the DIVINE HELPER uncovers merciless racist evil, they say TRUTHS supported by cogent and irrefutable evidence is CONSPIRACY THEORY.

WHICH PART OF HEREDITARY RACIAL HATRED AND FRAUD IS CONSPIRACY THEORY?

We are guilty because we cannot defend ourselves against hereditary RACIST pure white bastards before hereditary RACIST pure white bastard Judges – **Habakkuk 1:4.**

Then, they won in crooked courts before crooked Judges, but in the WAR when the Corporal flipped, the only sinless Judge looked away (**John 5:22**), and insatiably greedy RACIST BASTARDS lost everything and more.

If the facts do not fit the theory, change the facts: Ignorant hereditary RACIST pure white bastards (predominantly but not exclusively pure white), when their LIES do not fit their conspiracy theories, they change their lies, not their conspiracy theories: Seemingly, a variant of Mayor Giuliani's alternative truths, the Satanic New Name for Lies.

Lies are the new truths: "The truth allows no choice." Dr Samuel Johnson (1709 -1784).

Matthew 4:9: They do vulgar Pharisees' charitable works in exchange for what? Then, theirs was not a good deal, and it remains a very, very, very, bad deal. They are very, very, very, powerful in GREAT BRITAIN because it is illegal to deal with the hereditary RACIST pure white bastards (predominantly but not exclusively pure white) – **Exodus 21:23-27.** They should stay here, it is safer. There, we shall take revenge.

Matthew 12:46–50: Ina njo, ogiri ko sa: Some say they have the power to kill us **(Exodus 20:13)**, they should fu*king get on with it. We know what they do not know: X (any number) + infinity = infinity, so X=0.

"There is no hunting like the hunting of man, and those who have hunted armed men long enough and liked it, never care for anything else thereafter." Ernest Hemingway (1899–1961).

OYINBO OLE: "It was our arms in the river of Cameroon, put into the hands of the trader, that furnished him with the means of pushing his trade; and I have no more doubt that they are British arms, put into the hands of Africans, which promote universal war and desolation that I can doubt their having done so in that individual instance. I have shown how great is the enormity of this evil, even on the supposition that we take only convicts and prisoners of war. But take the subject in another way, and how does it stand? Think of 80,000 persons carried out of their native country by what we know not what means! For crimes imputed! For light or inconsiderable faults! For debts perhaps! For the crime of witchcraft! Or a thousand other weak or scandalous pretexts! Reflect on 80,000 persons annually taken off! There is something in the horror of it that surpasses all bounds of imagination."—Prime Minister William Pitt the Younger

OYINBO OLE: Then, armed insatiably greedy bastards, and those they armed, carried and sold millions of stolen children of defenceless poor people, including the pure black African ancestors of our IMPURE DUCHESS OF SUSSEX, Princess Ada Mazi Omu of Arochukwu, Princess Meghan Markle (43% Nigerian), and her impure children (<43% Nigerian)—**Habakkuk**, now THIEVES carry our own natural resources from our own AFRICA—**EXODUS 20:15.**

QUASI-PEONAGE: SUBSTITUTION IS FRAUDULENT EMANCIPATION.

"Moderation is a virtue only among those who are thought to have found alternatives." Dr Henry Kissinger (1923–2023).

OYINBO OLE: Colour-blind and transparent equality under their law is an unrealistic aspiration. Only fantasists, Utopians, and historical imbeciles expect overnight giant leaps. No people will ever voluntarily relinquish several centuries-old advantageous positions in exchange for NOTHING.

"The highest reach of injustice is to be deemed just when you are not." Plato

OYINBO OLE: "But no advance in wealth, no softening of manners, no reform or revolution has ever brought human equality a millimetre nearer. From the point of view of the Low, no historic change has ever meant much more than a change in the name of their masters." George Orwell (1903–1950).

Exodus 20:15: White Privilege guarded by White Supremacy is a variant of STEALING, it is a properly organised RACIST SCAM that needs to be shattered.

"White supremacy is real, and it needs to be shattered." Dr Cornel West

"Change occurs slowly. Very often a legal change might take place, but the cultural shift required to really accept its spirit lingers in the wings for decades." Sara Sheridan

Exodus 20:15: They know how to steal for their people, but they don't know how to repair their scatter-heads of their own pure white kindred (predominantly but not exclusively pure white)—**Habakkuk 1:4.**

HUGE YIELDS OF SLAVERY DECOMMISSIONED NATURAL SELECTION AND MADE IT POSSIBLE FOR MILLIONS OF INCESTUOUSLY CONCEIVED BASTARDS TO BREED MORE MILLIONS OF INCESTUOUSLY CONCEIVED BASTARDS: BEFORE SLAVERY, WHAT?

"This statement is about a series of letters and emails I have been recieving. I am the above named person. I live at an address provided to police. In this statement I will also mention XXXXXXXXXXXXXXXXXXXXXXXXX a leaseholder for a property I manage at my place work. I am the company director of DOBERN properties based in Ilford. These emails have been sent to my company email address of mail@debern.co.uk, and also letters have been sent to myself at our company ADDress of P.O BOX 1289, ILFORD, IG2 7XZ over the last Two and a half years, I have recieving a series of letters and emails from DR BAMGeLu. DR BAMGBELU is a leasholder for a property I manage at my place of work. Over the period of his leaseholding, DR BAmGelu has continually failed to pay arrears for the property. In march 2016 my company took DR to court and he was ordered to pay outstanding costs of around £20000 since that time and lead up to the case, DR BaMGBelu has been emailing me and posting me letters that are lengthy and accuses me repeatedly of being a racist in emails and letters tact are regularly Ten to twelve pages long, DR BAMGBELU. lists numerous quots from google searches all refrencing ham I am a bigot and a racist. The most recent letter I received from DR BAMGBELU opens with you are jealous and racist Evil combination you hate us we know it" he goes on to say "I would not have knowingly had anything to do with white supremicists." In the last email I recieved from him on 02/09/2016 DR BaMGBELU stated "you are restricted by poor Education within one of the least literate countries in the world". I would be perfectly happy for DR BAMGBElu to contact myself or my company if he has relevant enquiries to his lease holding, however these continuous letters and emails are causing me distress and I feel intimidated. I am not a racist and these accusatios make uncomfortable. All I want is to conduct between us in a normal manner. I want BambGlu to stop emailing me and sending me letters accusing me of being racist and harassing me." PURE WHITE, CROOKED, AND HEREDITARY RACIST MR ROBERT KINGSTON, SOLICITOR, ACCOUNTANT, AND COMPANY DIRECTOR

BRAINLESS TORTUOUS GIBBERISH: THEY ARE INNATELY VERY, VERY, VERY, WICKED BASTARDS, AND INDISCREET THIEVES – **EXODUS 20:15, HABAKKUK 1:4.**

BRAINLESS RACIST NONSENSE: "Yes, Sir, it does her honour, but it would do nobody else honour. I have indeed not read it all. But when I take up the end of a web, and find a packthread, I do not expect, by looking further, to find embroidery." Dr Samuel Johnson (1709–1784).

"Gentlemen, you are now about to embark on a course of studies which will occupy you for two years. Together, they form a noble adventure. But I would like to remind you of an important point. Nothing that you will learn in the course of your studies will be of the slightest possible use to you in after life, save only this, that if you work hard and intelligently you should be able to detect when a man is talking rot, and that, in my view, is the main, if not the sole, purpose of education." John Alexander Smith (1869–1939), Professor of Moral Philosophy

OYINBO OLE: No brain. Poor natural resources. Several centuries of STEALING and SLAVERY preceded their HUGE STOLEN INHERITANCE—**Habakkuk.**

BEDFORD, ENGLAND: Our own Mediocre, Wonky, Pure White Hereditary Racist, unashamedly functionally semi-illiterate, poly-educated poor man's son, a mere former debt-collector Solicitor in Norfolk/Norwich (5th Rate Partner), and the Senior Vice President of the Association of Her Majesty's District Judges, Bedford's District Judge Paul Robert Ayers, 3, St Paul's Square, MK 40 1SQ, it is not the TRUTH that daily dialogues with scatter-head PURE WHITE BASTARDS (predominantly but not exclusively PURE WHITE) is a proper Job.

They hate us, and we know. They hate our children more, but they do not know. We do not need Peter Herbert (OBE) to tell us about evil RACIST BASTARDS.

"The white man is the devil." Elijah Mohammed (1897–1975).

OYINBO OLE: They love only our own money: Then, they carried and sold millions of stolen children of defenceless poor people, including the pure black African ancestors of our IMPURE DUCHESS OF SUSSEX, Princess Ada Mazi Omu of Arochukwu, Princess Meghan Markle (43% Nigerian), and her impure children (<43% Nigerian), now THIEVES steal our own NATURAL RESOURCES from our own AFRICA - **Habakkuk.**

Based on several decades of very, very, very, proximate observations and direct experiences, hereditary RACIST pure white bastards, (predominantly but not exclusively pure white), are greedier than the grave, and like death, the insatiably greedy pure white bastards will never be satisfied—**Habakkuk 2:5.**

Severe DYSLEXIA could be part of Alzheimer's disease and atypical dementia.

Based on cogent, irrefutable, and available evidence, Pure White, Crooked, and Hereditary RACIST Robert Kingston, England Class Solicitor, Accountant, and Company Director, maliciously, and recklessly lied or he was pathologically confused when he stated, "DR BAMGBELU. lists numerous quots from google searches all refrencing ham I am a bigot and a racist."

Lots and lots of Britons are Jews.

AA: Jewish family kicked off a flight for having 'extremely offensive body odour'

Based on very, very, very, proximate contacts, Robert Kingston, Solicitor, Accountant, and Company Director, albeit England's Class, STANK. The pure white Briton had a distinct body odour.

"Britons stank." W.S.

Wole Soyinka, not William Shakespeare (1564–1616) should know - at least one of his wives, and some of his concubines were Britons.

Again, based on cogent, irrefutable, and available evidence, Pure White, Crooked, and Hereditary RACIST Robert Kingston, England Class Solicitor, Accountant, and Company Director, maliciously, and recklessly lied or he was pathologically confused when he stated, "The most recent letter I received from DR BAMGBELU opens with you are jealous and racist Evil combination you hate us we know it" he goes on to say "I would not have knowingly had anything to do with white supremicists."

Again, based on cogent, irrefutable, and available evidence, Pure White, Crooked, and Hereditary RACIST Robert Kingston, England Class Solicitor, Accountant, and Company Director, maliciously, and recklessly lied or he was pathologically confused when he stated, "In the last email I recieved from him on 02/09/2016 DR BaMGBELU stated "you are restricted by poor Education within one of the least literate countries in the world"

Based on several decades of very, very, very, proximate observations and direct experiences, their unashamedly MEDIOCRE Fish and Chips Justice System is irreparably FU*KED, it has foreseeably succumbed to INCEST, weakening of the common genetic pool, and associated physical and/or mental wonkiness, and hereditary white supremacist Freemason Senior Judges, and others, who make loads of MONEY from unashamed mediocrity and confusion PROP SHIT UP: Conflict of interest.

"A government that robs Peter to pay Paul can always depend on the support of Paul." George Bernard Shaw (1856–1950).

The report, by the OECD, warns that the UK needs to take significant action to boost the basic skills of the nation's young people. The 460-page study is based on the first-ever survey of the literacy, numeracy and problem-solving at work skills of 16 to 65-year-olds in 24 countries, with almost 9,000 people taking part in England and Northern Ireland to make up the UK results. The findings showed that England and Northern Ireland have some of the highest proportions of adults scoring no higher than Level 1 in literacy and numeracy—the lowest level on the OECD's scale. This suggests that their skills in the basics are no better than that of a 10-year-old.

AN IMBECILE: AN ADULT WITH THE BASIC SKILLS OF A CHILD.

Apart from creating cushy salaried jobs for Solicitors and Barristers who couldn't hack it in the very competitive real world (quasi-communism), what do imbeciles need very expensive administration of the law for – **Habakkuk 1:4**?

Adults with the basic skills of a foetus will succeed adults with the basic skills of a child; the former will need only food and shelter, not very, very, very, expensive administration of English Law.

"We have the power to turn against our creators." Dr Richard Dawkins

AN OPPORTUNIST RACIST PURE WHITE BASTARD WAS GRANTED THE PLATFORM TO DISPLAY HEREDITARY PREJUDICE – **HABAKKUK 1:4.**

He should fu*king stay here, it's safer.

Exodus 21:23–27: There, we will take revenge, and Sir, Keir Starmer wouldn't do anything about it.

Then, all Judges were pure white Freemasons, and most of them were thicker than a gross of planks - **Habakkuk.**

Abuse of TEMPORARY POWER is the fullest definition of EVIL.

"Those who have the POWER to do wrong with impunity seldom wait long for the will." Dr Samuel Johnson (1709-1784).

Exodus 20:15: Then, pure white Freemason judges who believed that daily dialogues with PURE WHITE IMBECILES (predominantly but not exclusively pure white adults with the basic skills of a child) were SCAMMERS, and those who demanded and accepted very, very, very, valuable considerations in exchange for daily dialogues with imbeciles were THIEVES (racketeers).

OYINBO OLE/ODE:ACCURATE SEERS: Then, they foresaw that BRITONS would be imbeciles, so they embarked on armed robbery and dispossession raids in AFRICA, and wherever they mercilessly slaughtered AFRICANS, they dispossessed them, and whenever they ROBBED our people (AFRICANS), they took possession, and they used huge yields of millions of stolen children of defenceless poor people, including the pure black African ancestors of our IMPURE DUCHESS OF SUSSEX, Princess Ada Mazi Omu of Arochukwu, Princess Meghan Markle (43% Nigerian), and her impure children (<43% Nigerian)—**Habakkuk**, to CREATE a very, very, very, LAVISH SOCIALIST ELDORADO for imbeciles, and they decommissioned natural selection, and they reversed progressive evolution, and they made it possible for millions of imbeciles to breed more millions of imbeciles.

"I emphasis the point." Our own Mediocre, Wonky, Pure White Hereditary Racist, unashamedly functionally semi-illiterate, poly-educated poor man's son, a mere former debt-collector Solicitor in Norfolk/Norwich (5th Rate Partner), and the Senior Vice President of the Association of Her Majesty's District Judges, Bedford's District Judge Paul Robert Ayers, 3, St Paul's Square, MK 40 1SQ.

BRAINLESS RACIST NONSENSE.

OUR IMBECILE HEREDITARY RACIST FREEMASON SENIOR JUDGE OF OUR EMPIRE OF STOLEN INHERITANCE—**HABAKKUK.**

"I don't want to talk grammar. I want to talk like a lady." George Bernard Shaw (1856–1950).

If the pure white bastard read his approved Judgement, he was a FOOL, and if he did not, he LIED as he implied that he did—**Habakkuk 1:4**. The poor pure white ancestors of his pure white mother and father were incompetent RACIST LIARS too, like the ancestors of King's School and Oxbridge-educated Lord Justice Charles Anthony Haddon-Cave, KC, a RACIST son of a very, very, very, rich TASMANIAN Economic Cannibal (**Mark 10:25**), and an impostor and an expert of deception (perception is grander than reality), and a closeted white supremacist descendant of DRUG LORDS (opium merchants of the Qing Dynasty), and a homie of Eton and Oxbridge-educated very, very, very, rich men's son (**Mark 10:25**), Archbishop Justin Welby, they were THIEVES (**Exodus 20:15**), and owners of stolen children of defenceless poor people, including the pure black African ancestors of our IMPURE DUCHESS OF SUSSEX, Princess Ada Mazi Omu of Arochukwu, Princess Meghan Markle (43% Nigerian), and her impure children (<43% Nigerian)—**Habakkuk**.

Bedford's District Judge Paul Robert Ayers, our hereditary RACIST pure white bastard will say that he made a mistake, of course he did, and had he not made too many mistakes at school and in life, in general, he might not have settled for daily dialogues with PURE WHITE IMBECILES (predominantly but not exclusively pure white) in a LOWER COURT in Bedford, and he might have practiced proper LAW in Strand.

OUR OWN MONEY. OUR OWN NIGERIA, SHELL'S DOCILE CASH COW SINCE 1956 (OLOIBIRI). GDC WAS ESTABLISHED IN 1956.

Facts are sacred and cannot be overstated.

Unlike Putin's Russia, there are no oil wells or gas fields in bland and colourless NORFOLK/NORWICH (Coastal Dole/the Departure Lounge of Life) and where the pure white father and mother our own Mediocre, Wonky, Pure White Hereditary Racist, unashamedly functionally semi-illiterate, poly-educated poor man's son, a mere former debt-collector Solicitor in Norfolk/Norwich (5th Rate Partner), and the Senior Vice President of the Association of Her Majesty's District Judges, Bedford's District Judge Paul Robert Ayers, 3, St Paul's Square, MK 40 1SQ, were born.

The very, very, very, highly luxuriant soil of FREEMASONS' KEMPSTON yields only FOOD, and there are no oil wells or gas fields in Bishop's Stortford. Bishop's Stortford Cecil Rhodes (1853–1902) was a Racist Pure White Bastard and a THIEF (**Exodus 20:15**)

Our own Mediocre, Wonky, Pure White Hereditary Racist, unashamedly functionally semi-illiterate, poly-educated poor man's son, a mere former debt-collector Solicitor in Norfolk/Norwich (5th Rate Partner), and the Senior Vice President of the Association of Her Majesty's District Judges, Bedford's District Judge Paul Robert Ayers, 3, St Paul's Square, MK 40 1SQ: The pure white MASON Judge is an opportunist RACIST BASTARD and a Criminal that was granted the platform to display hereditary prejudice – **Habakkuk 1:4.**

Bedford's District Judge Paul Robert Ayers, the most important part of the matter is MONEY, and our own MONEY, NIGERIA (oil/gas) is by far more relevant to the economic survival of his pure white father, his pure white mother, his pure white spouse, and his white children than bland and colourless NORTHAMPTON.

Based on several decades of very, very, very, proximate observations and direct experiences, the WEAPON of the pure white privileged dullard (predominantly but not exclusively pure white), the direct descendant of the father of LIES (**John 8:44, John 10:10**) is the mother of RACIST LIES, and their POWER is the certainty that all Judges would be PURE WHITE, and their hope is that they would be hereditary white supremacist bastards too—**Habakkuk 1:4.** OYINBO OLE: No brain. Poor natural resources. Several continuous centuries of stealing and SLAVERY preceded their HUGE STOLEN INHERITANCE—**Habakkuk.**

Leviticus 19:33–34: Hereditary RACIST pure white bastards (predominantly but not exclusively pure white) have INVENTED a brand-new method of killing foreigners. Trump evicts foreigners; racist pure white bastards kill foreigners, albeit hands-off: They start by CRIMINALLY annulling the formal education of our own people (AFRICANS), and they vindictively economically strangulate our own people (AFRICANS), and they sadistically overwhelm the minds of our people, and they viciously destroy the minds of our people (FOREIGNERS), and they mercilessly kill our people, albeit hands-off, with the mens rea hidden in the belly of the actus reus.

Google: Dr Richard Bamgboye, GP.

Google: Dr Anand Kamath. Dentist.

They LIED to their own mentally gentler WHITE CHILDREN (OECD) and the pure white IMBECILES they shepherd (predominantly but not exclusively pure white) that they are ultra-righteous GENIUSES, very, very, very, highly civilised, and SUPER-ENLIGHTENED, and they do everything, absolutely everything LEGALLY, including RACIAL HATRED and FRAUD—**Habakkuk 1:4.**

"When a stupid man is doing something he is ashamed of, he always declares that it is his duty." George Bernard Shaw (1856–1950).

Leviticus 19:33–34: Ultra-righteous hereditary RACIST pure white bastards always declare that they are doing their

LEGITIMATE DUTIES::They always start by attaching MERCILESS RACIST EVIL to foreigners, and they do RACIAL HATRED until it takes hold, and when it does, they instantly revert to LEGALITY: Rules-based, procedures, precedent, and statute, including INDISCREET RACIAL HATRED and FRAUD—**Habakkuk 1:4.**

OYINBO OLE: Our own MONEY. Our own NIGERIAN BABIES with huge oil wells and gas fields near their huts eat only 1.5/day in our own NIGERIA, a very, very, very, bellyful semi-illiterate pure white bastard, a mere poly-educated former debt-collector Solicitor in bland and colourless NORWICH (5th Rate partner), whose pure white father and mother have never seen CRUDE OIL, and whose pure white ancestors, including Robert Hibbert (1769–1849) of LUTON, and John Foster (1759–1832) of BEDFORD, were fed like battery hens with yields of millions of stolen children of defenceless poor people, including the pure black African ancestors of our IMPURE DUCHESS OF SUSSEX, Princess Ada Mazi Omu of Arochukwu, Princess Meghan Markle (43% Nigerian), and her impure children (<43% Nigerian)—**Habakkuk**, was our Senior District Judge in BEDFORD, Great Britain. Which part of our own SHITHOLE AFRICA is great?

TWO MEAL TICKETS: Which one of our PUTRID TUBES did our Born-Again Christian tell our own Mediocre, Wonky, Pure White Hereditary Racist, unashamedly functionally semi-illiterate, poly-educated poor man's son, a mere former debt-collector Solicitor in Norfolk/Norwich (5th Rate Partner), and the Senior Vice President of the Association of Her Majesty's District Judges, Bedford's District Judge Paul Robert Ayers, 3, St Paul's Square, MK 40 1SQ, and Freemasons at Brickhill Baptist Church she used to work for 0.5M?

OYINBO OLE: Our own Mediocre, Wonky, Pure White Hereditary Racist, unashamedly functionally semi-illiterate, poly-educated poor man's son, a mere former debt-collector Solicitor in Norfolk/Norwich (5th Rate Partner), and the Senior Vice President of the Association of Her Majesty's District Judges, Bedford's District Judge Paul Robert Ayers, 3, St Paul's Square, MK 40 1SQ, a brainless hereditary RACIST pure white bastard DISHONESTLY implied that he did not know that SLAVERY rebuilt EVERYTHING it succeeded and paid for EVERYTHING it preceded, including Bedfordshire Masonic Centre MK42 8AH,and Bedford County Court, MK40 1SQ.

They don't want their own mentally gentler WHITE CHILDREN (OECD) and the pure white IMBECILES they shepherd (predominantly but not exclusively pure white)n to know the TRUTH, which is that apart from our INFERIOR SKIN COLOUR, which we neither made nor chose, and our FOREIGN ACCENT of speaking a FOREIGN LANGUAGE, our own people (AFRICANS), are also properly created by Almighty God, so to save face, hereditary RACIST pure white bastards (predominantly but not exclusively pure white) CRIMINALLY steal yields of our own people's Christ-granted talents, secure in the knowledge that all Judges would be PURE WHITE, and their hope is that they would be hereditary white supremacist bastards too—**Habakkuk**.

Facts are sacred and cannot be overstated: "Find the truth and tell it." Harold Pinter (1930-2008).

BEDFORD, ENGLAND: GDC, Crooked, Hereditary RACIST, and Pure White Bastard, Richard William Hill, England's Class Senior NHS Postgraduate Tutor, Bedfordshire, fabricated and unrelentingly lied under oath and on record—**Habakkuk 1:4**. The poor pure white ancestors of his pure white father and mother were incompetent RACIST LIARS too, like the ancestors of King's School and Oxbridge-educated Lord Justice Charles Anthony Haddon-Cave, KC, a RACIST son of a very, very, very, rich TASMANIAN Economic Cannibal (**Mark 10:25**), an impostors and an expert of deception (perception is grander than reality), and a closeted white supremacist descendant of DRUG LORDS (opium merchants of the Qing Dynasty), and a homie of Eton and Oxbridge-educated very, very, very, rich men's son (**Mark 10:25**), Archbishop Justin Welby, they were THIEVES (**Exodus 20:15**), and owners of stolen children of defenceless poor people, including the pure black African ancestors of our IMPURE DUCHESS OF SUSSEX, Princess Ada Mazi Omu of Arochukwu, Princess Meghan Markle (43% Nigerian), and her impure children (<43% Nigerian)—**Habakkuk**.

A very, very, very, DISHONEST typical pure white Englishman. A crooked closeted hereditary RACIST Freemason.

Exodus 20:15: If you are brainless, your land is natural resources poor, and you are very rich, your ancestors must have been THIEVES—**Habakkuk.**

BEDFORD, ENGLAND: Our own Mediocre, Wonky, Pure White Hereditary Racist, unashamedly functionally semi-illiterate, poly-educated poor man's son, a mere former debt-collector Solicitor in Norfolk/Norwich (5th Rate Partner), and the Senior Vice President of the Association of Her Majesty's District Judges, Bedford's District Judge Paul Robert Ayers, 3, St Paul's Square, MK 40 1SQ, it is not the TRUTH that daily dialogues with IMBECILES is a proper job. Your ancestors were Racist Murderers (Exodus 20:13), PROFESSIONAL THIEVES (**Exodus 20:15**), and owners of stolen children of defenceless poor people, including the pure black African ancestors of our IMPURE DUCHESS

OF SUSSEX, Princess Ada Mazi Omu of Arochukwu, Princess Meghan Markle (43% Nigerian), and her impure children (<43% Nigerian)—**Habakkuk**.

"Sometimes people don't want to hear the truth because they don't want their illusions destroyed." F4riedrich Nietzsche (1844–1900).

OYINBO OLE: Equitable, fair, and just reparation pends, and several centuries of unpaid interest accrue.

"They may not have been well written from a grammatical point of view, but I am confident I had not forgotten any of the facts." Crooked, Hereditary Racist, and Pure White Welsh bastard, Geraint Evans, England's Class Welsh Postgraduate Tutor, Oxford.

Part of the resultant effects of several continuous centuries of stealing and slavery is that a pure white Welsh imbecile was our Senior Postgraduate Tutor, Oxford. They foresaw that a pure white Welsh imbecile would be our Senior Postgraduate Tutor, Oxford, so they embarked on armed robbery and dispossession raids in AFRICA: Whenever they mercilessly slaughtered AFRICANS, they dispossessed them, and wherever they robbed our own direct ancestors (AFRICANS), they took possession, and HUGE GAINS of several continuous centuries of Stealing, Slavery. Colonisation, and Neocolonialism—made it possible to pay a crooked, hereditary RACIST, and pure white Welsh imbecile the salary of a Senior Postgraduate Tutor, Oxford.

OYINBO ODE: Part of the reasons why the GDP of the USA is about 300X bigger than that of WALES (>$30trillion: >0.1<$0.125 trillion), is because a crooked, hereditary racist, and pure white Welsh imbecile was paid the salary of a Senior Postgraduate Tutor, Oxford.

******

Case No: 2YL06820

Bedford County Court

May House

29 Goldington Road

Bedford

MK40 3NN

Monday, 1st July 2013

B E F O R E:

DISTRICT JUDGE AYERS

DOBERN PROPERTY LIMITED

(Claimants)

v.

DR. ABIODUN OLA BAMGBELU

(Defendant)

Transcript from an Official Court Tape Recording.

Transcript prepared by:

MK Transcribing Services

29 The Concourse, Brunel Business Centre,

Bletchley, Milton Keynes, MK2 2ES

Tel: 01908–640067 Fax: 01908–365958

DX 100031 Bletchley

Official Court Tape Transcribers.

MR. PURKIS appeared on behalf of THE CLAIMANTS.

THE DEFENDANT appeared in PERSON.

PROCEEDINGS OF MONDAY, 1ST JULY 2013

Monday, 1st July 2013

DISTRICT JUDGE AYERS: Mr. Purkis, you weren't here, I know, on the last occasion representing the claimants, but we had a very long hearing concerning the lease. There's a letter from Mr. Bamgbelu dated 6th June, which I don't know whether you have seen.

MR. PURKIS: Yes, sir.

DISTRICT JUDGE AYERS: In that case it seems to me it's over to you to prove your case.

MR. PURKIS: Sir, it continues to be our case that we rely on the lease and the terms of the lease that have been put forward. On the last occasion, my understanding was that it was—in essence it was accepted by the court that those terms were likely to be terms between the parties that were entered into, and I'm referring to the lease contained in the bundle. Mr. Bamgbelu was therefore required to dispute that, in essence, by providing a copy of a lease that he said contained the appropriate terms.

DISTRICT JUDGE AYERS: What I actually said to him, and I went through this numerous times with him, was that the copy of the lease that you produced was the one at the Land Registry, it happened to be the one signed by the landlord, and he was saying that that wasn't the one that was signed by him. He said he had solicitors at the time who advised him, and pressing very hard about it, and on numerous occasions, he insisted that he wished to go back to his solicitors then and find a copy of the lease that they had that they advised him on, and to check that against the copy that you have. The letter, as you see, simply says that he doesn't accept that, and it's up to you to produce a copy signed by him. Well, the position is very very clear this afternoon. I made a very clear order on the last occasion that if he didn't produce any evidence to challenge the validity of your lease, as your lease was registered at the Land Registry, I would accept that even if he would not be in a position to challenge what that lease contained. End of story. He is stuck with that lease. All I want to do today is to hear evidence from you as to the amount outstanding.

MR. PURKIS: Thank you, sir.

MR. BAMGBELU: Am I allowed to say something, sir?

DISTRICT JUDGE AYERS: No. Do you wish to—— -

MR. BAMGBELU: It is not fair, sir.

DISTRICT JUDGE AYERS: Mr. Bamgbelu, do you wish to say anything about that particular issue?

MR. BAMGBELU: Yes, sir.

DISTRICT JUDGE AYERS: What do you wish to say?

MR. BAMGBELU: The lease that I read and signed, when you sign the lease, sir, it is exchanged. The only lease that I read and signed—— -

DISTRICT JUDGE AYERS: No, Mr. Bamgbelu, let me explain this to you.

MR. BAMGBELU: That'—— -

DISTRICT JUDGE AYERS: It is up to the claimants to prove their case. They have produced a copy of the lease that is registered at the Land Registry. That is a lease and they are able to prove their case on that. The fact that they have not got your copy or the copy signed by you, is neither here nor there, because the importance is the document which is registered at the Land Registry, and investigations say that it is a copy signed by the landlord which has to be placed at the Land Registry. I made that perfectly clear to you on the last occasion.

MR. BAMGBELU: That's—— -

DISTRICT JUDGE AYERS: You were the one who challenged that that lease was not an accurate copy of the lease that you've signed.

MR. BAMGBELU: I did not say that, sir.

DISTRICT JUDGE AYERS: Yes, you did.

MR. BAMGBELU: I did not say that, sir.

DISTRICT JUDGE AYERS: I was here the last occasion——— -

MR. BAMGBELU: I did not say that, sir.

DISTRICT JUDGE AYERS:———that is exactly what you said.

MR. BAMGBELU: What I said, sir, was that I am happy to accept that.

DISTRICT JUDGE AYERS: No, you weren't.

MR. BAMGBELU: I said that.

DISTRICT JUDGE AYERS: Mr. Bamgbelu, you cannot argue with me, I was here, because I was at some—— -

MR. BAMGBELU: Okay.

DISTRICT JUDGE AYERS: ——— considerable length to go through that with you, because you kept saying——— -

MR. BAMGBELU: I said——— -

DISTRICT JUDGE AYERS: ——— that, and I said if you accept——— -

MR. BAMGBELU: I accepted it, sir.

DISTRICT JUDGE AYERS: ——— if you accept that lease as the lease, then we didn't need to go any further. You insisted on having the matter adjourned so you could go——— -

MR. BAMGBELU: I did not do that, sir.

DISTRICT JUDGE AYERS: ——— and get—okay.

MR. BAMGBELU: Yes.

DISTRICT JUDGE AYERS: Well, okay, we'll disagree on that then, but I can remember full well what I said——— -

MR. BAMGBELU: I have a very good memory, sir.

DISTRICT JUDGE AYERS: ——— and if necessary——— -

MR. BAMGBELU: As well as (Inaudible).

DISTRICT JUDGE AYERS: ——— if necessary I will have the tape played back to you——— -

MR. BAMGBELU: Yes, yes.

DISTRICT JUDGE AYERS: ——— that's exactly what is said.

MR. BAMGBELU: Okay.

MR. PURKIS: The claim is for £320.66 service charge.

DISTRICT JUDGE AYERS: Well, you'd better, I think, call your client or Mrs. Thomas to give evidence, to deal with the issues that are outstanding.

MR. PURKIS: Certainly, sir. May I call Mrs. Thomas?

Mrs. L. Thomas

Examined by Mr. Purkis.

Q. Mrs. Thomas, you have a bundle in front of you, and I believe that if you turn to page 141, you'll see a document there that says at the top, 'Witness statement of Lisa Thomas.' Is that your witness statement?

A. That's correct.

Q. If we turn to paragraph 8 there, it says, 'In the circumstances, I respectfully ask the court to enter judgment for the amount claimed of £410.66,' then it says, 'which comprises of the court fee for issuing the claim, totalling £95, and solicitors fees on issuing of £80.' Can I confirm that those fees of £95 and £80 aren't in fact included in that £410.66?

A. No, there is an error.

DISTRICT JUDGE AYERS: Right. Before we go any further, Mr. Purkis, we'd better have your client telling me who she is.

MR. PURKIS: Very well, sir. Could you give your full name to the court?

A. My name is Mrs. Lisa Jane Thomas, I'm property manager for Residential Block Management Services, and our clients are Dobern Properties.

Q. And how long have you been managing this particular block?

A. From around December 2010 when we was instructed by the previous agents. They were the administrators.

MR. BAMGBELU: Do you have proof of that?

******

BRAINLESS RACIST NONSENSE.
BEDFORD, ENGLAND: District Judge Paul Robert Ayers, which part of Bedford Masonic Centre, MK42 8AH, and Bedford County Court MK40 1SQ, was not STOLEN, or which part did your own pure white father and mother buy, or which part preceded SLAVERY?

OYINBO OLE: YOUR ANCESTORS WERE THIEVES – **HABAKKUK.**

They were all pure white: Archie is impure, <43% Nigerian.

Homogeneity in the administration of English Law is the impregnable secure mask of merciless RACIST EVIL— **Habakkuk 1:4; John 8:44; John 10:10.**

Their unashamedly MEDIOCRE Fish and Chips Justice System subjugates colour blind-merit and propagates Apartheid by stealth.

JUDICIAL DIVERSITY: ACCELERATING CHANGE. Sir Geoffrey Bindman, QC, and Karon Monaghan, QC: "The near absence of women and Black, Asian and minority ethnic judges in the senior judiciary, is no longer tolerable. It undermines the democratic legitimacy of our legal system; it demonstrates a denial of fair and equal opportunities to members of underrepresented groups, and the diversity deficit weakens the quality of justice."

Racist Suppression of Evidence: The Senior Judge, albeit England's Class, did not want his pure white kindred, Mrs Lisa Thomas, England's Class Manager, to expatiate on 'AN ERROR', so he dishonestly implied that he did not know who she was, and constructively changed the trajectory of the cross-examination, and CRIMINALLY BURIED THE TRUTH.

Google: The White Judge Lied.

UK justice system is racist, suggests one of Britain's only …

https://www.independent.co.uk › UK › Home News

10 Jan 2017—At the same event, Mr Herbert also suggested ethnic minorities "should not place their faith in a justice system that had not been designed …

At the hearing and before the hearing, the name of the Negro was different from the name on the Transcript of the hearing of July 01, 2013.

The closeted racist white cretins seemed to believe that the Negro created the name Bamgbela—for some sinister purposes.

They neither knew nor understood their people, so they grossly overrated them.

BEDFORD, ENGLAND: Based on cogent, irrefutable, and available evidence, our own Mediocre, Wonky, Pure White Hereditary Racist, unashamedly functionally semi-illiterate, poly-educated poor man's son, a mere former debt-collector Solicitor in Norfolk/Norwich (5th Rate Partner), and the Senior Vice President of the Association of Her Majesty's District Judges, Bedford's District Judge Paul Robert Ayers, 3, St Paul's Square, MK 40 1SQ, LIED under oath (approved Judgement) when he explicitly stated that the NIGERIAN was invited to, and took part in, a hearing at

Bedford County Court, May House, 29, Goldington, Road, Bedford,MK40 3NN, Monday, 1st July 2013—**Habakkuk 1:4.** The poor pure white ancestors of his pure white father and mother were incompetent RACIST LIARS too, like the ancestors of King's School and Oxbridge-educated Lord Justice Charles Anthony Haddon-Cave, KC, a RACIST son of a very, very, very, rich Tasmanian Colonialist Economic Cannibal (**Mark 10:25**), an impostor and an expert of deception (perception is grander than reality), and a closeted white supremacist descendant of DRUG LORDS (opium merchants of the Qing Dynasty), and a homie of Eton and Oxbridge-educated Archbishop Justin Welby, a closeted white supremacist very, very, very, rich men's son (**Mark 10:25**), they were THIEVES (**Exodus 20:15**), extremely nasty RACIST MURDERERS (**Exodus 20:13**), and owners of stolen children of defenceless poor people, including the pure black African ancestors of our IMPURE DUCHESS OF SUSSEX, Princess Ada Mazi Omu of Arochukwu, Princess Meghan Markle (43% Nigerian), and her impure children (<43% Nigerian)—**Habakkuk**.

BEDFORD, ENGLAND: Our own Mediocre, Wonky, Pure White Hereditary Racist, unashamedly functionally semi-illiterate, poly-educated poor man's son, a mere former debt-collector Solicitor in Norfolk/Norwich (5th Rate Partner), and the Senior Vice President of the Association of Her Majesty's District Judges, Bedford's District Judge Paul Robert Ayers, 3, St Paul's Square, MK 40 1SQ, the supernatural exists, and it is consistently accessible to those who stand where it can come (**John 14:26**). Reasoning and vision do not have finite boundaries. Hereditary RACIAL HATRED is not a myth, and it is considerably more common than ordinarily realised. We do not need Peter Herbert (OBE) to preach to us about the MERCILESS RACIST EVIL our people (Africans) endure daily, in their Godforsaken RACIST HELL HOLE—**Habakkuk 1:4**. The mind that I did not choose is FINER than your unashamedly MEDIOCRE Fish and Chips Justice System, and I do not believe in ant part of SHIT, as no part of SHIT is good, not even one—**Psalm 53,** and I have the POWER to use cogent facts and irrefutable evidence to irreparably destroy you and SHIT—**Habakkuk 1:4.**

The centuries-old unspoken myth that intellect is related to the universally acknowledged irrefutably SUPERIOR SKIN COLOUR that the very, very, very, very, fortunate wearer neither made nor chose is the mother of all RACIST SCAMS.

OYINBO OLE: BEDFORD, ENGLAND: Crooked, Hereditary Racist, and Pure White Mere DMF, Sue Gregory (OBE) unrelentingly lied under implied oath and on record—**Habakkuk 1:4.** The poor pure white ancestors of her pure white father and mother were incompetent RACIST LIARS too, like the ancestors of King's School and Oxbridge-educated Lord Justice Charles Anthony Haddon-Cave, KC, a RACIST son of a very, very, very, rich Tasmanian Colonialist Economic Cannibal (**Mark 10:25**), an impostor and expert of deception (perception is grander than reality), and a closeted white supremacist descendant of DRUG LORDS (opium merchants of the Qing Dynasty), and a homie of Eton and Oxbridge-educated Archbishop Justin Welby, a closeted white supremacist very, very, very, rich men's son (**Mark 10:25**), they were THIEVES (**Exodus 20:15**), extremely nasty RACIST MURDERERS (**Exodus 20:13**), and owners of stolen children of defenceless poor people, including the pure black African ancestors of our IMPURE DUCHESS OF SUSSEX, Princess Ada Mazi Omu of Arochukwu, Princess Meghan Markle (43% Nigerian), and her impure children (<43% Nigerian)—**Habakkuk.**

A very, very, very, DISHONEST typical pure white Englishwoman. A crooked closeted hereditary RACIST Officer of the Most Excellent Order of our Empire of Stolen Inheritance – **Habakkuk.**

BEDFORD, ENGLAND: Our own Mediocre, Wonky, Pure White Hereditary Racist, unashamedly functionally semi-illiterate, poly-educated poor man's son, a mere former debt-collector Solicitor in Norfolk/Norwich (5th Rate Partner), and the Senior Vice President of the Association of Her Majesty's District Judges, Bedford's District Judge Paul Robert Ayers, 3, St Paul's Square, MK 40 1SQ, in our own NIGERIA, our own Nigerian babies with huge oil wells and gas fields near their eat only 1.5/day, in our own NIGERIA, but over here, a very, very, very, bellyful semi-illiterate PURE WHITE BASTARD, a mere poly-educated poor man's son, and a former debt-collector Solicitor in bland and colourless NORWICH (lowlife 5th Rate Partner), whose pure white mother and father have never seen CRUDE OIL, and whose pure white ancestors, including ultra-righteous John Bunyan (1628–1688), and Italian Jewish ancestors of Benjamin Disraeli (1804–1881), were fed like battery hens with huge yields of millions of stolen children of defenceless poor people, including the pure Black African ancestors of the IMPURE (<43% Nigerian) of the great grandchildren of the Duke of Edinburgh of Blessed Memory, Prince Phillip (1921–2021), was our Senior District Judge in Bedford, Great Britain. Which part of our shithole Africa is great?

Lord Leon Brittan (1939-2015): "A German Jew." Lord Denning (1899-1999).

THREE: Philippians 1:21: Phillip was a 33rd Degree Freemason (Scottish Rite).

Our own Mediocre, Wonky, Pure White Hereditary Racist, unashamedly functionally semi-illiterate, poly-educated poor man's son, a mere former debt-collector Solicitor in Norfolk/Norwich (5th Rate Partner), and the Senior Vice President of the Association of Her Majesty's District Judges, Bedford's District Judge Paul Robert Ayers, 3, St Paul's Square, MK 40 1SQ: You are a very, very, very, hardened opportunist RACIST pure white bastard. You are consumed by innate ENVY and hereditary RACIAL HATRED.

Colonial Mentality: When HEREDITARY RACIAL HATRED and familial intellectual impotence unravels, the only defence available to hereditary RACIST pure white bastards is INSANITY. Any NEGRO who disagrees with any member of their brainlessly and baselessly self-awarded SUPERIOR RACE is MENTAL: Neo-colonialism.

"To disagree with three-fourths of the British public on all points is one of the first requisites of sanity, one of the deepest consolations in all moments of spiritual doubt." Wilde (1854–1900).

Their hairs stand on end when they are challenged by our people, AFRICANS; we and our type are the only one's hereditary RACIST PURE WHITE BASTARDS would beat up without the support of the YANKS.

"Ethical Foreign policy." Robin Cook (1946–2005).

Psalm 118:22, Luke 20:17: If the BUILDERS are as ethical and as brave as they brag, they must, DIRECTLY, use overwhelming extreme violence to evict PUTIN from Crimea; he used extreme overwhelming violence to convert

Bakhmut from bricks to rubble and stole it—**Exodus 20:15.**

OYINBO OLE: FLAT TRACK BULLIES. TRUMP'S POODLES.

GOOGLE: IMAGBON, 1892.

Our own Mediocre, Wonky, Pure White Hereditary Racist, unashamedly functionally semi-illiterate, poly-educated poor man's son, a mere former debt-collector Solicitor in Norfolk/Norwich (5th Rate Partner), and the Senior Vice President of the Association of Her Majesty's District Judges, Bedford's District Judge Paul Robert Ayers, 3, St Paul's Square, MK 40 1SQ: You and your type are not the only creation of Almighty God, and you are not immortal, and the universally acknowledged irrefutably SUPERIOR SKIN COLOUR that you neither made nor chose is not the only wonder of our world.

Proverbs 20:15: Skin colour is a great creation of Almighty God, but it is not the greatest.

The centuries-old unspoken myth that intellect is related to the universally acknowledged irrefutably SUPERIOR SKIN COLOUR that the very, very, very, fortunate wearer neither made nor chose—is the mother of all RACIST SCAMS.

OYINBO OLE/ODE: Our own Mediocre, Wonky, Pure White Hereditary Racist, unashamedly functionally semi-illiterate, poly-educated poor man's son, a mere former debt-collector Solicitor in Norfolk/Norwich (5th Rate Partner), and the Senior Vice President of the Association of Her Majesty's District Judges, Bedford's District Judge Paul Robert Ayers, 3, St Paul's Square, MK 40 1SQ, our own MONEY, Nigeria (oil/gas), is by far more relevant to the economic survival of all your own mentally gentler WHITE CHILDREN (OECD). There, you would be found, and

SUMMARILY DEALT WITH, and legally—within the native and customary law – **Exodus 21:23-27.**

Dr Mungo Park (1771–1806) had guns. Unlike him, you wouldn't be killed, but you would be sold by descendants of those who were carried and sold by your ancestors – during several continuous centuries of merciless RACIST EVIL, the greediest economic cannibalism and the evilest RACIST TERRORISM the world would ever know – **Habakkuk 2:5.**

"We shall deal with the racist bastards when we get out of prison." Comrade Robert Mugabe (1924–2019).

Based on several decades of very, very, very, proximate observations and direct experiences, they are innately very, very, very, wicked bastards—**Habakkuk 1:4.**

We do not need Quasi-Pastors, PETER HERBERT (OBE) and Sir, Bernard Hogan-Howe, KBE, to preach to us about Institutionalised MERCILESS RACIST EVIL that we experience – in their Godforsaken RACIST HELL HOLE, almost daily.

UK justice system is racist, suggests one of Britain's only …

https://societyofblacklawyers.co.uk › uk-justice-system-…

Britain's justice system is racist and should not be trusted by ethnic minorities, one of the UK's only black judges has suggested. Peter Herbert, a part-time …

"All sections of UK society are institutionally racist." Sir, Bernard Hogan-Howe, KBE.

Facts are sacred and cannot be overstated.

They DECEIVED their own mentally gentler WHITE CHILDREN (OECD) and pure white imbeciles they shepherd (predominantly but not exclusively pure white) that our own people (AFRICANS) are Inferior Creation of

Almighty God, and to conceal the TRUTH, which is that apart our INFERIOR SKIN COLOUR and our foreign accent of speaking a foreign language, we are also properly created by Almighty God, they CRIMINALLY steal yields of our own people's (AFRICANS) Christ-granted talents, secure in the knowledge that all JUDGES would be pure white, and their hope is that they would all be hereditary white supremacist bastards too – **Habakkuk 1:4.**

OXFORD, ENGLAND, BRITISH SOLDIER: GDC, Crooked, Hereditary Racist, and Pure White Bastard, Stephanie Twidale (TD) unrelentingly lied under oath and on record—**Habakkuk 1:4.** The poor pure white ancestors of her pure white father and mother were incompetent RACIST LIARS too, like the ancestors of King's School and Oxbridge-educated Lord Justice Haddon-Cave, KC, a RACIST son of a very, very, very, rich Tasmanian Colonialist Economic Cannibal (**Mark 10:25**), an impostor and an expert of deception (perception is grander than reality), and a closeted white supremacist descendant of DRUG LORDS (opium merchants of Qing Dynasty), and a homie of Eton and Oxbridge-educated very, very, very, rich men's son (**Mark 10:25**), ARCHBISHOP JUSTIN WELBY, they were THIEVES and owners of stolen children of defenceless poor people, including the pure black African ancestors of our IMPURE DUCHESS OF SUSSEX, Princess Ada Mazi Omu of Arochukwu, Princess Meghan Markle (43% Nigerian), and her impure children (<43% Nigerian)—**Habakkuk.**

A very, very, very, DISHONEST typical pure white Englishwoman. A crooked closeted hereditary RACIST British Soldier (Territorial Defence). Had she been IMPURE, she would have been in trouble. Meghan Markle is impure, <43% Nigerian.

A brainless pure white pig: "I am very fond of my pigs, but that does not stop me from eating them." Archbishop Runcie (1921–2000).

If one farmed WHITE PIGS, with great snouts. in the African bush, the stupidest of the white pigs, with great snouts, deserves to be killed, and eaten first.

"There is no sin except stupidity." Wilde (1854-1900).

"Meghan was the victim of explicit and obnoxious racial hatred." John Bercow, a former speaker.

The YANKS are NATO, and absolutely everything else is an auxiliary bluff.

BEDFORD, ENGLAND: Our own Mediocre, Wonky, Pure White Hereditary Racist, unashamedly functionally semi-illiterate, poly-educated poor man's son, a mere former debt-collector Solicitor in Norfolk/Norwich (5th Rate Partner), and the Senior Vice President of the Association of Her Majesty's District Judges, Bedford's District Judge Paul Robert Ayers, 3, St Paul's Square, MK 40 1SQ, sincere immodesty is sincerer than insincere modesty: You are INFERIOR. You are WORTHY only because the pure white ancestors of your pure white mother and father were extremely nasty merciless racist murderers (**Exodus 20:13**), nastier than Yevgeny Prigozhin (1961–2023), INDUSTRIAL-SCALE PROFESSIONAL THIEVES (**Exodus 20:15**), immoral drug dealers (opium merchants of the Qing Dynasty), and owners of stolen children of defenceless poor people, including the pure Black African ancestors of the IMPURE (<43% Nigerian) niece and nephew of the Prince of Wales— Habakkuk. Before SLAVERY, what? It is absolutely impossible to compete on a colour-blind level playing field without resorting to RACIST CRIMINALITY. Had you been a NIGG*R, and thrice as smart, you wouldn't be a Judge. A brainless hereditary RACIST pure white bastard. A mere poly-educated former debt-collector Solicitor in NORWICH was granted the platform to display hereditary prejudice—**Habakkuk 1:4.**

The universally acknowledged irrefutably SUPERIOR SKIN COLOUR that the very, very, very, fortunate wearer neither made nor chose, a HUGE STOLEN INHERITANCE—**Habakkuk,** and what else? Before Slavery, what? Then, there was only subsistence feudal agriculture.

"Agriculture not only gives riches to a nation, but the only one she can call her own." Dr Samuel Johnson (1709–1784).

OYINBO OLE/ODE, 1976–2022: Our own Mediocre, Wonky, Pure White Hereditary Racist, unashamedly functionally semi-illiterate, poly-educated poor man's son, a mere former debt-collector Solicitor in Norfolk/Norwich (5th Rate Partner), and the Senior Vice President of the Association of Her Majesty's District Judges, Bedford's District Judge Paul Robert Ayers, 3, St Paul's Square, MK 40 1SQ, a brainless hereditary RACIST pure white bastard, an impostor, and an expert of deception, having FAILED in practice (loads did), the opportunist RACIST pure white bastard, a mere lowlife poly-educated (not Russell Group Inferior Class Alternative Education—**Proverbs 17:16**), former debt-collector Solicitor in bland and colourless NORFOLK/NORWICH (5th Rate Partner) parked his liability at the public till (where else), and the hereditary RACIST pure white bastard sold unashamed mediocrity and confusion to the undiscerning. Only his universally acknowledged irrefutably SUPERIOR SKIN COLOUR and Almighty God are truly good (**Mark 10:18**), and he neither made nor chose it, and he would be considerably diminished as a human being without it, and the opportunist RACIST evil bastard knows it.

EXODUS 21:23–27: THE CROOKED BRAINLESS PURE WHITE BASTARD SHOULD FU*KING STAY HERE, IT IS SAFER.

"Stoning certainly teaches people a lesson." Supreme Court Justice, Ayatollah Sadegh Khalkhali (1926–2003).

Then, in our own tribe in the AFRICAN BUSH, the hereditary RACIST pure white bastard would have been treated with sticks and stones, loads of them.

Our own Mediocre, Wonky, Pure White Hereditary Racist, unashamedly functionally semi-illiterate, poly-educated poor man's son, a mere former debt-collector Solicitor in Norfolk/Norwich (5th Rate Partner), and the Senior Vice President of the Association of Her Majesty's District Judges, Bedford's District Judge Paul Robert Ayers, 3, St Paul's Square, MK 40 1SQ: An ignorant one-dimensionally educated descendant of THIEVES dishonestly implied that he did not know that the PURE WHITE ANCESTORS of his own pure white father and mother were THIEVES— **Habakkuk,** and he also dishonestly implied that he did not know that SLAVERY rebuilt everything it succeeded and paid for everything it preceded, including Bedford County Court, MK40 1SQ, and Bedfordshire Masonic Centre, MK42 8AH, and our opportunist RACIST pure white bastard further dishonestly implied that he did not know that equitable, fair, and just reparation pends, and several centuries of unpaid interest accrue.

"Who am I to Judge?" Pope Francis (1936–2025).

John 5:22: BEDFORD, ENGLAND, Our own Mediocre, Wonky, Pure White Hereditary Racist, unashamedly functionally semi-illiterate, poly-educated poor man's son, a mere former debt-collector Solicitor in Norfolk/Norwich (5th Rate Partner), and the Senior Vice President of the Association of Her Majesty's District Judges, Bedford's

District Judge Paul Robert Ayers, 3, St Paul's Square, MK 40 1SQ, God Judges no one.

John 5:22: Only He who has no sin has the MORAL RIGHT to Judge sinners. A functional semi-illiterate hereditary RACIST pure white bastard, a very, very, very, hardened EVIL descendant of THIEVES and owners of stolen children of defenceless poor people, including the pure black African ancestors of our IMPURE DUCHESS OF SUSSEX, Princess Ada Mazi Omu of Arochukwu, Princess Meghan Markle (43% Nigerian), and her impure children (<43% Nigerian)—**Habakkuk**, does not have the MORAL RIGHT to Judge Sinners—as he is neck deep in personal and inherited sins—**John 8:7, Matthew 7:1–6**.

"Blue-eyed devils." Elijah Mohammed (1897–1975).

Matthew 12:27: Blue-eyed devils cannot cast out green-eyed demons.

The pattern of MERCILESS RACIST EVIL is the same everywhere in their Godforsaken Racist Hell Hole.

"Racism is rife throughout most organisations across Britain." Sir, Sadiq Khan, KBE.

Facts are Holy; repetitive TRUTHS should be HOLIER: "Find the truth and tell it." Harold Pinter (1930-2008).

BEDFORD, ENGLAND: Our own Mediocre, Wonky, Pure White Hereditary Racist, unashamedly functionally semi-illiterate, poly-educated poor man's son, a mere former debt-collector Solicitor in Norfolk/Norwich (5th Rate Partner), and the Senior Vice President of the Association of Her Majesty's District Judges, Bedford's District Judge Paul Robert Ayers, 3, St Paul's Square, MK 40 1SQ, I neither believe nor respect any part of your unashamedly MEDIOCRE Fish and Chips Justice System—**Habakkuk 1:4**. The mind that I did not choose is FINER than SHIT, and no part of SHIT is good, not even one—**Psalm 53,** and I have the POWER to use cogent facts and irrefutable evidence to irreparably destroy you and every part of SHIT—**Habakkuk 1:4.**

OYINBO OLE/ODE: Our own Mediocre, Wonky, Pure White Hereditary Racist, unashamedly functionally semi-illiterate, poly-educated poor man's son, a mere former debt-collector Solicitor in Norfolk/Norwich (5th Rate Partner), and the Senior Vice President of the Association of Her Majesty's District Judges, Bedford's District Judge Paul Robert Ayers, 3, St Paul's Square, MK 40 1SQ. a brainless hereditary RACIST pure white bastard deceived his own mentally gentler white children (OECD) and the pure white IMBECILES he shepherds (predominantly but not exclusively pure white) that his nomination and constructive appointment by dementing or demented pure white FREEMASON LORDS was based on colour-blind and progressive measurable objectivity, and he concealed the TRUTH, which is that the last time he passed through the filter of measurable objectivity was when he studied 5th Rate Law at Poly, and it showed.

"This man I thought had been a Lord among wits, but I find he is only a wit among Lords." Dr Samuel Johnson (1709–1784).

"Should 500 men, ordinary men, chosen accidentally from among the unemployed, override the judgement—the deliberate judgement—of millions of people who are engaged in the industry which makes the wealth of the country?" David Lloyd George (1863–1945).

WHITE PRIVILEGE: WHITE SUPREMACISTS' SCAM.

Our unashamedly functional semi-illiterate poly-educated pure white bastard looked like a son of a plebeian hoe from

Eastern Europe, with an arbitrarily acquired camouflage English name.

The opportunist RACIST pure white bastard gave the game away when he approved and immortalised what his pure white mumsy spoke, albeit a mere plebeian hoe from Eastern Europe—with an arbitrarily acquired camouflage English name, and which his poly-educated superiors and supervisors in LUTON authorised.

HHJ Perusko studied law at Poly: Not Russell Group Inferior Class Alternative Education—Proverbs 17:16.

HHJ Perusko (CROATIA), Michael Portillo (SPAIN), Yinka Bamgbelu (NIGERIA), Mohammed Al Fayed (EGYPT), and Ali Kemal (TURKEY) did not arbitrarily acquire camouflage English names.

Saxe-Coburg, and Gotha, family changed their name in 1917.

Gustav Liebson (1876–1947) arbitrarily acquired a camouflage English name in 1925, and had he not, Nigel Lawson (1932 – 2023) would not have been our Chancellor.

Ján Ludvík Hyman Binyamin Hoch (1923–1991) was Ghislaine Maxwell's dad. Had the Jew not arbitrarily acquired a camouflage British name; his daughter might have been found out earlier.

Had Ali Kemal (1867–1922) been as rich as Mohammed Al Fayed (1929–2023), Boris Johnson would have been Mohammed Ali, and he would not have been our PREMIER.

Gigantic yields of millions of stolen children of defenceless poor people, not feudal agriculture, lured Eastern European Jews to Great Britain. Before Slavery, what?

"A German Jew." Oxbridge-educated very, very, very, rich draper's son (**Mark 10:25**), Lord Denning (1899–1999), an unapologetic hereditary white supremacist descendant of THIEVES and owners of Stolen Children of Defenceless Poor AFRICANS - **Habakkuk.**

The Jewish ancestors of Sir Malcolm Rifkind and his cousin, Lord Denning (1939–2015)—were economic migrants from Eastern Europe (Lithuania).

OYINBO OLE/ODE: Then, RACIST PURE WHITE BASTARDS carried and sold millions of stolen children of defenceless poor people, now THIEVES steal our own natural resources from our own AFRICA.

SUBSTITUTION IS FRAUDULENT EMANCIPATION.

"Moderation is a virtue only among those who are thought to have found alternatives." Dr Henry Kissinger (1923–2023).

THE CARRYING TRADE IS IMMORTAL - **HABAKKUK.**

In monetary terms, what very, very, very, greedy racist bastards carry now (>$200 billion/Annum) is worth considerably more than the tens of millions of other people's stolen children evil racist bastards carried and sold (1445–1888).

HOUSE OF LORDS: Then, Alzheimer's disease and Atypical Dementia were very, very, very, common in the UPPER CHAMBER.

Alzheimer's disease and/or atypical dementia are incompatible with the competent administration of English Law. The competent administration of English Law is an inviolable basic right.

OYINBO OLE/ODE: Our own Mediocre, Wonky, Pure White Hereditary Racist, unashamedly functionally semi-illiterate, poly-educated poor man's son, a mere former debt-collector Solicitor in Norfolk/Norwich (5th Rate Partner), and the Senior Vice President of the Association of Her Majesty's District Judges, Bedford's District Judge Paul Robert Ayers, 3, St Paul's Square, MK 40 1SQ, a brainless hereditary RACIST pure white bastard was granted the platform to display HEREDITARY PREJUDICE— **Habakkuk 1:4.**

BEDFORD, ENGLAND: Our own Mediocre, Wonky, Pure White Hereditary Racist, unashamedly functionally semi-illiterate, poly-educated poor man's son, a mere former debt-collector Solicitor in Norfolk/Norwich (5th Rate Partner), and the Senior Vice President of the Association of Her Majesty's District Judges, Bedford's District Judge Paul Robert Ayers, 3, St Paul's Square, MK 40 1SQ, apart from debt-collection, what was in bland and colourless NORFOLK/NORWICH (Coastal Dole/ the Departure Lounge of Life) for pure white Freemason Solicitors to do (predominantly but not exclusively pure white).

OYINBO OLE/ODE: Our own Mediocre, Wonky, Pure White Hereditary Racist, unashamedly functionally semi-illiterate, poly-educated poor man's son, a mere former debt-collector Solicitor in Norfolk/Norwich (5th Rate Partner), and the Senior Vice President of the Association of Her Majesty's District Judges, Bedford's District Judge Paul Robert Ayers, 3, St Paul's Square, MK 40 1SQ, a brainless hereditary RACIST pure white bastard sat on a very, very, very, expensive HIGHCHAIR that his own pure white father and mother could not afford, and which the pure white IMBECILES (predominantly but not exclusively pure white) who sat before him could not, and did not, buy, in a GRAND COURT that was preceded by Slavery, future flats, and absolutely inevitable distant future Nuclear Ash, and

Judged SINNERS: 29, Goldington Road. MK40 3NN, is a block of flats.

JOHN 8:7, MATTHEW 7:1–6: A BRAINLESS HEREDITARY RACIST PURE WHITE BASTARD, A VERY, VERY, VERY, VERY, HARDENED OPPORTUNIST WHITE SUPREMACIST EVIL SENIOR JUDGE OF PURE WHITE IMBECILES (PREDOMINANTLY BUT NOT EXCLUSIVELY PURE WHITE), SAT ON THE BONES OF STOLEN CHILDREN OF DEFENCELESS POOR AFRICANS (MORE BONES THAN THE MILLIONS OF SKULLS AT THE DOORSTEP OF POL POT (1925–1998), AND FROM THE THRONE, THE OPPORTUNIST RACIST PURE WHITE BASTARD JUDGED SINNERS—**REVELATION 3:21, REVELATION 20: 11–15.**

John 5:22: God Almighty Judges no one, but only He has the MORAL RIGHT to appoint Judges, and only He who has no sin has the MORAL RIGHT to Judge sinners— **Matthew 25:31–46:** Our own Mediocre, Wonky, Pure White Hereditary Racist, unashamedly functionally semi-illiterate, poly-educated poor man's son, a mere former debt-collector Solicitor in Norfolk/Norwich (5th Rate Partner), and the Senior Vice President of the Association of Her Majesty's District Judges, Bedford's District Judge Paul Robert Ayers, 3, St Paul's Square, MK 40 1SQ, a Racist pure white bastard, a mere poly-educated former debt-collector Solicitor (lowlife 5th Rate Partner) was granted the platform to display hereditary prejudice. The opportunist RACIST PURE WHITE BASTARD did not have the MORAL RIGHT to Judge SINNERS because he is a descendant of THIEVES (**Exodus 20:15**): Extremely nasty and merciless Racist Murderers (**Exodus 20:13**), nastier than Yevgeny Prigozhin (1961–2023) and HITLER (1889–1945), several years of NAZI HOLOCAUST (1939–1945) was a mere storm in a teacup in comparison to MAAFA. A very, very, very, hardened opportunist RACIST descendant of industrial-scale professional armed robbers, armed land grabbers, Gun Runners, Drug Dealers (Opium Merchants of the Qing Dynasty), and owners of stolen children of defenceless poor people, including the pure black African ancestors of our IMPURE DUCHESS OF SUSSEX, Princess Ada Mazi Omu of Arochukwu, Princess Meghan Markle (43% Nigerian), and her impure children (<43% Nigerian)—**Habakkuk**.

Our own Mediocre, Wonky, Pure White Hereditary Racist, unashamedly functionally semi-illiterate, poly-educated poor man's son, a mere former debt-collector Solicitor in Norfolk/Norwich (5th Rate Partner), and the Senior Vice President of the Association of Her Majesty's District Judges, Bedford's District Judge Paul Robert Ayers, 3, St Paul's Square, MK 40 1SQ, a brainless hereditary RACIST pure white bastard. Only his SUPERIOR SKIN COLOUR and GOD are truly good—**Mark 10:18.**

Facts are sacred and they cannot be overstated.

1976–2022: Our own Mediocre, Wonky, Pure White Hereditary Racist, unashamedly functionally semi-illiterate, poly-educated poor man's son, a mere former debt-collector Solicitor in Norfolk/Norwich (5th Rate Partner), and the Senior Vice President of the Association of Her Majesty's District Judges, Bedford's District Judge Paul Robert Ayers, 3, St Paul's Square, MK 40 1SQ, a brainless opportunist hereditary white supremacist bastard FAILED in practice, loads did, and he parked his liability at the PUBLIC TILL, and sold unashamed MEDIOCRITY and confusion to the undiscerning—**Habakkuk 1:4.**

Part of the reasons why the GDP of USA is about 10X bigger than that of the UK (>$30 trillion: >$3 trillion < $4 trillion) is because a pure white functional semi-illiterate bastard, a mere former debt-collector Solicitor in bland and colour

NORWICH (5th Rate Partner) was paid the salary of a Senior Judge, >£200,000/Annum. Having FAILED in practice, loads did, the opportunist RACIST PURE WHITE BASTARD parked his liability at the public till, where else?

QUASI-COMMUNISM: Then, when Solicitors and Barristers FAILED in practice, loads did, if they were FREEMASONS, they became Judges or something else, if not, they became POLITICIANS, or something else.

"Someone must be trusted, let it be the Judges." Lord Denning (1899–1999).

Hereditary White Supremacist Judges are human beings: Some human beings are RACISTS.

RACIAL BIAS ANDTHE BENCH

https://www.criminalbar.com › uploads › 2023/02

PDF

In fact, there are currently no Black judges in the High. Court, Court of Appeal or Supreme Court. Not one. As Judge Peter Herbert stated: "The judiciary is …

Based on several decades of very, very, very, proximate observations and direct experiences, their unashamedly MEDIOCRE Fish and Chips Justice System is irreparably FU*KED, it has foreseeably succumbed to INCEST, weakening of the common genetic pool, and associated physical and/or mental wonkiness, and hereditary white supremacist SENIOR JUDGES, and others, who make loads of money from unashamed mediocrity and confusion PROP SHIT UP—**Habakkuk 1:4:** Conflict of Interest.

"A government that robs Peter to pay Paul can always depend on the support of Paul." George Bernard Shaw (1856–1950).

BEDFORD, ENGLAND: Our own Mediocre, Wonky, Pure White Hereditary Racist, unashamedly functionally semi-illiterate, poly-educated poor man's son, a mere former debt-collector Solicitor in Norfolk/Norwich (5th Rate Partner), and the Senior Vice President of the Association of Her Majesty's District Judges, Bedford's District Judge Paul Robert Ayers, 3, St Paul's Square, MK 40 1SQ, your pure white ancestors were Racists, Murderers, THIEVES, and owners of stolen children of defenceless poor people, including the pure black African ancestors of our IMPURE DUCHESS OF SUSSEX, Princess Ada Mazi Omu of Arochukwu, Princess Meghan Markle (43% Nigerian), and her impure children (<43% Nigerian)—**Habakkuk**, and you 'a blood sucker', with all the characteristics of an IMPUDENT SCOTTISH LEECH. The most important part of the matter is MONEY, and it is not the yield of your talent, and unlike PUTIN'S RUSSIA, there are no oil wells or gas fields in FREEMASONS' NORTHAMPTON and where you own pure white father and mother were born.

"The impudence of an Irishman is the impudence of a fly, that buzzes about you, and you put it away, but it returns and flutters and teases you. The impudence of a Scotsman is the impudence of a leech, that fixes and sucks your blood." Dr Samuel Johnson (1709–1784).

John 14:26: Bedford, England, Our own Mediocre, Wonky, Pure White Hereditary Racist, unashamedly functionally semi-illiterate, poly-educated poor man's son, a mere former debt-collector Solicitor in Norfolk/Norwich (5th Rate Partner), and the Senior Vice President of the Association of Her Majesty's District Judges, Bedford's District Judge Paul Robert Ayers, 3, St Paul's Square, MK 40 1SQ, let me tell you, the SUPERNATURAL exists, and it is consistently accessible to those who stand where it can come. Reasoning and vision do not have FINITE BOUNDARIES. The fellow is who He says He is—**John 14:6**.

Acts 2:17: I am a FOETUS, as what I can vividly see is clearer than dreams, visions, and prophecies.

John 5:22: There is only one TRUE JUDGE, and He sees all and knows all—**Proverbs 15:3,** and He will Judge all, including CROOKED FREEMASON JUDGES, with the Sword of TRUTH, not Jonathan Aitken's, but the Divine Sword of Transparent TRUTH.

Genetic damage is the most enduring residue of several centuries of European Christians' sadistic commerce in millions of stolen children of defenceless poor people (Kamala's ancestors)—**Habakkuk**.

Percentage of children in the UK hitting educational targets at 5, in descending order:

1. Asian (Indian)

2. Asian (Any other Asian)

3. White (British)

4. White (Irish)

5. Mixed (any other)

6. Mixed (white and black African)

7. Chinese

8. Mixed (White and black Caribbean)

9. Black (African heritage)

10. Asian (Any other Asian)

11. Black (Caribbean heritage)

12. Black (other)

13. Asian (Bangladeshi)

14. White (Any other white)

15. Any other ethnic group

16. Asian (Pakistani)

17. White (Traveller of Irish heritage)

18. White (Gypsy/ Roma)

Source: Centre Forum, 2016

Children in the UK hitting educational targets at 16, in descending order:

1. Chinese

2. Asian (Indian)

3. Asian (Any other Asian)

4. Mixed (White and Asian)

5. White (Irish)

6. Mixed (Any other)

7. Any other ethnic group

8. Asian (Bangladeshi)

9. Parent/pupil preferred not to say

10. Mixed (White and black African)

11. White (Any other white)

12. Black (African heritage)

13. White (British)

14. Asian (Pakistani)

15. Black (other)

16. Mixed (White and black Caribbean)

17. Black (Caribbean heritage)

18. White (Traveller of Irish heritage)

19. White (Gypsy/ Roma)

Source: Centre Forum, .2016

"Pardon him, Theodotus: he is a barbarian, and thinks that the customs of his tribe and Island are the laws of nature." George Bernard Shaw.

Barbaric decapitation was removed from the statute book in 1973; the last decapitation in Great England was in 1817.

Their people are very compliant; some of them are like zombies. Extremely nasty bastards have systematically tamed the compliant genes and ruthlessly deselected the brighter non-compliant genes with open beheading in Market Squares.

COLOURISM: BRAINLESSLY AND BASELESSLY SELF-AWARDED INTELLECTUAL SUPERIORITY OF THE SUPERIOR RACE.

If Yellow People (Chinese) whose children were first of the list of those meeting academic targets at age 16, were granted the basic right to choose, they wouldn't choose white Britons whose children were thirteenth on the list of those meeting academic targets at age 16, why should our own people, NIGERIANS (AFRICANS) whose children were above white Britons on the list of those meeting academic targets at age 16, allow a pure white Gypsy-Like Senior Judge—guide the education of their Negro children—when PURE WHITE GYPSIES were last on the list of those meeting academic targets at age 16?

Mark 10:25: Elon Musk: Hereditary Intra-Racial Sex Machine.

FOUR: Elon Musk, you do simultaneous equations with only one set of equations; you are a spiritual IMBECILE—**John 14:26.**

New Herod, **Matthew 2:16:** Hereditary RACIST pure white bastards (predominantly but not exclusively pure white) see molecules and they destroy all those who see quarks.

Matthew 19:21: Elon Musk, you are worthy only because you are PURE WHITE, and worthier because you are the RICHEST PERSON in this finite reality, but you shan't be in the succeeding infinite reality because you shan't be there—**Mark 10:25.** Finite Reality + Infinite Reality = Infinite Reality. Finite Reality is a HOLE in the AIR, PURIFIED NOTHING.

Elon Musk, the supernatural exists and it is consistently accessible to those who stand where it can come—John **14:26.**

Sheep unnaturally shepherd sheep. Shepherds know that sheep are morons, but sheep do not know that shepherds are morons too.

"Mediocrity weighing mediocrity in the balance, and incompetence applauding its brother………" Wilde (1854–1900).

Elon Musk, let me tell you, the fact that A>B isn't proof that A and B are not crap, as better than crap could also be crap, and any finite relative to any finite is SHIT relative to infinite: purified nothing. Everything that is not aligned with the NOTION of infinity, the dimension of infinite reasoning and vision depicted by **John 14:6**, is intellectually flawed.

Reasoning and vision do not have finite boundaries, and anything that does not have TRUTH based on infinite reasoning and vision—is intellectually flawed.

"Tyrannical Police State." Elon Musk. How else should LUNATICS and IMBECILES be controlled?

"The best argument against democracy is a five-minute conversation with the average voter." Sir Winston Churchill (1874–1965).

Conflict of interest: Elon Musk, let me tell you, based on cogent, irrefutable, and available evidence, their unashamedly MEDIOCRE Fish and Chips Justice System is irreparably FU*KED, it has foreseeably succumbed to INCEST, weakening of the common genetic pool, and associated physical and/or mental wonkiness, and hereditary white supremacist FREEMASON JUDGES, and others, who make loads of MONEY from unashamed mediocrity and confusion prop shit up—**Habakkuk 1:4.**

"A government that robs Peter to pay Paul can always depend on the support of Paul." George Bernard Shaw (1856–1950).

Bedford's District Judge Ayers: White Skin and Stolen Trust …

https://www.amazon.co.uk › Bedfords-District-Judge-A…

Buy Bedford's District Judge Ayers: White Skin and Stolen Trust Fund. Before Slavery, What?: 100% Genetic Nigerian Whistleblowing Mole by Ekweremadu, …

£8.19

BEDFORD, ENGLAND: DISTRICT JUDGE PAUL ROBERT AYERS, YOU ARE TRAPPED: YOU ARE A RACIST CRIMINAL; I HAVE EVIDENCE – **HABAKKUK 1:4.**

Google: The White Judge Lied.

BEDFORD, ENGLAND: GDC, Crooked, Hereditary Racist, and Pure White Bastard, Freemason, Brother Richard William Hill fabricated reports and unrelentingly lied under oath and on record – **Habakkuk 1:4.**

When Hereditary RACIAL HATRED is unravelled by the HELPER (**John 14:26**), it instantly mutates to a CONSPIRACY THEORY, or Hereditary RACIST pure white bastards (predominantly not exclusively pure white) will baselessly and brainlessly declare that the WITNESS and/or VICTIM of merciless RACIST EVIL is mental, as it is absolutely impossible for members of their brainlessly and baselessly self-awarded superior race to be RACIST CRIMINALS – **Habakkuk 1:4.**

"He has refused to submit to a medical examination." King's School and Oxbridge-educated Lord Justice Charles Anthony Haddon-Cave, KC, a RACIST son of a very, very, very, rich TASMANIAN COLONIALIST ECONOMIC CANNIBAL (**Mark 10:25**), Oxbridge-educated rich man's son, Sir Charles Phillip Haddon-Cave (1925-1999) – who has been inside HELL FIRE since 1999, and his first son will absolutely inevitably join him there.

Matthew 14: King's School and Oxbridge-educated Lord Justice Charles Anthony Haddon-Cave, KC, a RACIST son of a very, very, very, rich TASMANIAN COLONIALIST ECONOMIC CANNIBAL (**Mark 10:25**), Oxbridge-educated rich man's son, Sir Charles Phillip Haddon-Cave (1925-1999), was John jailed because he lied, or did the intolerant LUNATIC JEW remove his head because he was mental?

Matthew 27:32-56: King's School and Oxbridge-educated Lord Justice Charles Anthony Haddon-Cave, KC, a

RACIST son of a very, very, very, rich TASMANIAN COLONIALIST ECONOMIC CANNIBAL (**Mark 10:25**), Oxbridge-educated rich man's son, Sir Charles Phillip Haddon-Cave (1925-1999), was Jesus lynched like Gadhafi because He lied, or was He crucified because He was mental?

"Jesus is the bedrock of my faith." HM (1926-2022).

OYINBO OLE/ODE: AN IGNORANT HEREDITARY WHITE SUPREMACIST DESCENDANT OF ULTRA-RIGHTEOUS PURE WHITE THIEVES AND OWNERS STOLEN CHILDREN OF DEFENCELESS POOR PEOPLE (AFRICANS) – **HABAKKUK.**

OXFORD, ENGLAND: GDC, Crooked, Hereditary Racist, and Pure White Bastard, British Soldier, Stephanie Twidale (TD) unrelentingly lied under oath and on record – **Habakkuk 1:4.**

BEDFORD, ENGLAND: Our own Mediocre, Wonky, Pure White Hereditary Racist, unashamedly functionally semi-illiterate, poly-educated poor man's son, a mere former debt-collector Solicitor in Norfolk/Norwich (5th Rate Partner), and the Senior Vice President of the Association of Her Majesty's District Judges, Bedford's District Judge Paul Robert Ayers, 3, St Paul's Square, MK 40 1SQ, it is not the TRUTH that daily dialogues with pure white IMBECILES (predominantly but not exclusively pure white) is a proper job that is worthwhile and manly. No brain. Poor natural resources. Several continuous centuries of STEALING and SLAVERY preceded their huge STOLEN INHERITANCE—**Habakkuk.**

"Affluence is not a birth right." Lord Cameron.

PERCEPTION IS GRANDER THAN REALITY.

OYINBO OLE/ODE: AN IGNORANT HEREDITARY RACIST DESCENDANT OF ULTRA-RIGHTEOUS PURE WHITE THIEVES AND OWNERS OF STOLEN CHILDREN OF DEFENCELESS POOR PEOPLE (AFRICANS)—**HABAKKUK.**

"They may not have been well written from a grammatical point of view but I am confident I had not forgotten any of the facts." Crooked, Hereditary Racist, and pure white WELSH IMBECILE, Geraint Evans, England's Class Welsh Postgraduate Tutor, Oxford.

OYINBO ODE: OUR PURE WHITE WELSH IMBECILE OF OUR EMPIRE OF STOLEN INHERITANCE— **HABAKKUK, EXODUS 20:15.**

Their type killed the INDIAN, only 42, and the NIGERIAN, only 56, albeit hands-off with the mens rea in the belly of the actus reus.

Google: Dr Anand Kamath, Dentist.

Google: Dr Richard Bamgboye, GP.

Exodus 21:23–27: They should fu*king stay here, it is safer. There, we shall remove a tooth for a tooth and accept the consequence, any.

"The earth contains no race of human beings so totally vile and worthless as the Welsh............" Walter Savage Landor (1775–1864).

Unlike PUTIN'S RUSSIA, there are no oil wells or gas fields in the VALLEYS, including NICK GRIFFIN'S Llanerfyl Powys, and where the pure white father and mother of Crooked, Hereditary Racist, and pure white WELSH IMBECILE, Geraint Evans, England's Class Welsh Postgraduate Tutor, Oxford, were born.

BEDFORD, ENGLAND: Our own Mediocre, Wonky, Pure White Hereditary Racist, unashamedly functionally semi-illiterate, poly-educated poor man's son, a mere former debt-collector Solicitor in Norfolk/Norwich (5th Rate Partner), and the Senior Vice President of the Association of Her Majesty's District Judges, Bedford's District Judge Paul Robert Ayers, 3, St Paul's Square, MK 40 1SQ, a brainless hereditary RACIST pure white bastard was granted the platform to display hereditary prejudice, and he ultra-righteously sat on a very, very, very, expensive HIGHCHAIR that his own pure white father and mother couldn't afford, and which the pure white IMBECILES (predominantly but not exclusively pure white) who sat before him couldn't, and didn't, buy, in their very, very, very, grand court that was preceded by SLAVERY, future flats and absolutely inevitable distant future's NUCLEAR ASH (29, Goldington Road, MK40 3NN, is a block of flats), and the opportunist RACIST pure white bastard, who is NECK DEEP in personal and inherited sins, a RACIST descendant of THIEVES **(Exodus 20:15)**: Extremely nasty and merciless RACIST MURDERERS **(Exodus 20:13)**, nastier than YEVGENY PRIGOZHIN (1961–2023), and eviler than the Austrian Corporal (1889–1945), and the functional semi-illiterate poly-educated lowlife son of NOBODIES Judged SINNERS—**John 8:7, Matthew 7:1–6**.

BEDFORD, ENGLAND: District Judge Paul Robert Ayers, our lowlife pure white bastard was granted the platform to display hereditary prejudice—**Habakkuk 1:4**. No brain. Poor natural resources. Several centuries of stealing and slavery preceded their huge STOLEN INHERITANCE—**Habakkuk**. Before SLAVERY, what? Then, there was only subsistence feudal agriculture.

OYINBO OLE/ODE: "Agriculture not only gives riches to a nation, bit the only one she can call her own." Dr Samuel Johnson (1709–1784).

Facts are sacred and cannot be overstated.

John 5:22: Only SAINTS have the Moral Right to Judge Sinners. Descendants of Immoral Economic Cannibals, and Opium Merchants of the Qing Dynasty, do not have the MORAL RIGHT to Judge sinners – **Matthew 7:1-6, John 8:7.**

Elon Musk, hereditary intra-racial sex machine, let me tell you, we are all who we are, the inheritors of our inheritances, genes of our individual ancestor. Several years of NAZI HOLOCAUST (1939–1945) was a mere storm in a teacup in comparison to MAAFA (1445–1888).

"Blue-eyed devils." Elijah Mohammed (1897–1975).

Matthew 12:27: it is not the TRUTH that blue-eyed devils can cast out green-eyed demons.

"I have seen evil, and it has the face of Mark Fuhrman." Johnnie Cochran (1937–2005).

Elon Musk, you are PURE WHITE, but Archie is not (<43% Nigerian), and like Mark Fuhrman, Bedford's District Judge Paul Robert Ayers - is PURE WHITE. Poly-educated pure white rubbish: Superior Skin Colour, a huge stolen inheritance, and what else? Before Slavery, what?

MARK 10:25: BEDFORD'S DISTRICT JUDGE PAUL ROBERT AYERS: OYINBO OLE/ODE: A RACIST DESCENDANT OF ULTRA-RIGHTEOUS INDUSTRIAL-SCALE PROFESSIONAL DRUG DEALERS (OPIUM MERCHANTS OF THE QING DYNASTY).

Google: Opium War, 1839–1842.

Google: Opium Trade, 1844–1912.

UK justice system is racist, suggests one of Britain's only ...

https://www.independent.co.uk › UK › Home News

10 Jan 2017—At the same event, Mr Herbert also suggested ethnic minorities "should not place their faith in a justice system that had not been designed.

OYINBO OLE/ODE: Properly rehearsed ultra-righteousness and deceptively schooled civilised decorum were preceded by several continuous centuries of MERCILESS RACIST EVIL: The greediest economic cannibalism and evilest, and the most violent RACIST TERRORISM the world will ever know—**Habakkuk.**

Habakkuk 2:5: Based on several decades of very, very, very, proximate observations and direct experiences, they are greedier than the grave, and like death, the hereditary RACIST pure white bastard (predominantly but not exclusively pure white) can never be satisfied.

"England is like a prostitute who, having sold her body all her life, decides to close her business, and then tells everybody she wants to be chaste and protect her flesh as if it were jade." He Manzi (1919–2009).

They see a LORD JUSTICE, but the NIGERIAN, from shithole Africa, sees a grossly overrated son of a very, very, very, RICH Tasmanian Colonialist Economic Cannibal (Mark 10:25), Sir Charles Phillip Haddon-Cave (1925–1999), and an impostor and an expert of deception (perception is grander than reality), and a closeted white supremacist descendant of DRUG LORDS (opium merchants of the Qing Dynasty), who owes everything, absolutely everything, to unearned privileges and undeserved patronages; if they are not excessively stupid, I must be MENTAL.

"To disagree with three-fourths of the British public on all points is one the first requisites of sanity, one of the deepest consolations in all moments of spiritual doubt." Wilde (1854-1900).

Then, in our own AFRICAN BUSH, Crooked, Hereditary Racist, and pure white WELSH IMBECILE, Geraint Evans, England's Class Welsh Postgraduate Tutor, Oxford, would not be carried, not only because he is physically ill-favoured, but more because he is mentally wonky.

Letters of a Racist Crooked Imbecile Welsh Dentist, Geraint …

https://www.amazon.co.uk › Letters-Crooked-Imbecile-…

Geraint. R. Evans—BDS (Bham), MSc GDP, Cert Clin Ed, Cert Implant: Letters and Lies of a Crooked Racist Welsh Imbecile. Google: Mediocre GDC.

£10.44

Helen Falcon (MBE), Member of the Most Excellent Order of our Empire of Stolen Inheritance reminded the NIGERIAN, from shit hole Africa, of Welsh Prostitutes a Scottish Poet mingled with.

"The ordinary women of Wales are generally short and squat, ill-favoured, and nasty." David Mallet (1705–1765).

New Herod, **Matthew 2:16:** They lied to their own mentally gentler WHITE CHILDREN (OECD) and the pure white IMBECILES they shepherd (predominantly but not exclusively pure white) that they are ULTRA-RIGHTEOUS GENIUSES, who do everything LEGALLY: Rules Based Procedures (CPR), Statute, Precedent Etcetera, including RACIAL HATRED and FRAUD, and they 'kill' (destroy) foreigners who know they are not.

Leviticus 19:33–34: The Nigerian, only 56, and Indian, only 42, were unlawfully killed, albeit hands-off, with the mens rea hidden in the belly of the actus reus: They are worse than TRUMP: Trump evicts foreigners, including children; here, hereditary RACIST pure white bastards (predominantly not exclusively pure white) kill foreigners.

Google: Dr Richard Bamgboye, GP.

Google: Dr Anand Kamath, Dentist

Exodus 21:23–27: Racist bastards should stay here, it is safer. There, we shall take revenge.

"We shall deal with the racist bastards when we get out of prison." Comrade Robert Mugabe (1924–2019).

OUR OWN NIGERIA, SHELL'S DOCILE CASH COW SINCE 1956 (OLOIBIRI). GDC WAS ESTABLISHED IN 1956.

OYINBO OLE: Unlike PUTIN'S RUSSIA, there are no oil wells or gas fields in bland and colourless NORFOLK/NORWICH (Coastal Dole/ the Departure Lounge of life) and where the pure white mother and father of our own Mediocre, Wonky, Pure White Hereditary Racist, unashamedly functionally semi-illiterate, poly-educated poor man's son, a mere former debt-collector Solicitor in Norfolk/Norwich (5th Rate Partner), and the Senior Vice President of the Association of Her Majesty's District Judges, Bedford's District Judge Paul Robert Ayers, 3, St Paul's Square, MK 40 1SQ, were born.

"I emphasis the point." Our own Mediocre, Wonky, Pure White Hereditary Racist, unashamedly functionally semi-illiterate, poly-educated poor man's son, a mere former debt-collector Solicitor in Norfolk/Norwich (5th Rate Partner), and the Senior Vice President of the Association of Her

Majesty's District Judges, Bedford's District Judge Paul Robert Ayers, 3, St Paul's Square, MK 40 1SQ.

"I don't want to talk grammar. I want to talk like a lady." George Bernard Shaw (1856–1950).

A brainless hereditary RACIST pure white bastard was granted the platform to display hereditary prejudice, and opportunist RACIST pure white bastard approved and immortalised what his pure white father and mother spoke, which his poly-educated pure white superiors and supervisors in LUTON authorised—**Habakkuk 1:4.**

HHJ Perusko studied law at POLY: Not Russell Group Inferior Class Alternative Education—**Proverbs 17:16.**

OUR IMBECILE, UNASHAMEDLY FUNCTIONAL SEMI-ILLITERATE, AND HEREDITARY RACIST FREEMASON SENIOR JUDGE OF OUR OWN EMPIRE OF STOLEN INHERITANCE—**HABAKKUK.**

Our own Mediocre, Wonky, Pure White Hereditary Racist, unashamedly functionally semi-illiterate, poly-educated poor man's son, a mere former debt-collector Solicitor in Norfolk/Norwich (5th Rate Partner), and the Senior Vice President of the Association of Her Majesty's District Judges, Bedford's District Judge Paul Robert Ayers, 3, St Paul's Square, MK 40 1SQ: If our brainless hereditary RACIST pure white bastard read his approved Judgement, he was a FOOL. and if he did not, he lied as he implied that he did—**Habakkuk 1:4**. The poor pure white ancestors of his pure white mother and father were incompetent RACIST LIARS too, like the ancestors of King's School and Oxbridge-educated Lord Justice Charles Anthony Haddon Cave, KC, a RACIST son of a very, very, very, rich Tasmanian Colonialist Economic Cannibal (**Mark 10:25**), an impostor and an expert of deception (perception is grander than reality), and a hereditary white supremacist descendant of DRUG LORDS (opium merchants of the Qing Dynasty), and a homie of Eton and Oxbridge-educated RICH MEN'S SON, Archbishop Justin Welby **(Mark 10:25)**, they were THIEVES and owners of stolen children of defenceless poor people, including the pure black African ancestors of our IMPURE DUCHESS OF SUSSEX, Princess Ada Mazi Omu of Arochukwu, Princess Meghan Markle (43% Nigerian), and her impure children (<43% Nigerian)—**Habakkuk.**

ALL COLONIALIST, INCLUDING SIR CHARLES PHILLIP HADDON-CAVE, (1925–1999), WERE THIEVES: NEO-COLONIALISM IS ANOTHER VARIANT OF STEALING—**EXODUS 20:15.**

"The colonialists care nothing for Africa for her own sake. They are attracted by African riches and their actions are guided by the desire to preserve their interests in Africa against the wishes of the African people. For the colonialists all means are good if they help them to possess these riches" Patrice Lumumba (1925–1961).

"Negro is a stage in the slow evolution from monkeys to man." Dr Frantz Fanon (1925–1961).

"We are no longer your monkeys." Patrice Lumumba (1925–1961).

OUR OWN NIGERIA, SHELL'S DOCILE CASH COW SINCE 1956 (OLOIBIRI): GDC WAS ESTABLISHED IN 1956.

Unlike PUTIN'S RUSSIA, there are no oil wells or gas fields in bland and colourless NORFOLK/NORWICH (Coastal Dole/the Departure Lounge of life) and where the pure white father and mother of our own Mediocre, Wonky, Pure White Hereditary Racist, unashamedly functionally semi-illiterate, poly-educated poor man's son, a mere former debt-collector Solicitor in Norfolk/Norwich (5th Rate Partner), and the Senior Vice President of the Association of Her Majesty's District Judges, Bedford's District Judge Paul Robert Ayers, 3, St Paul's Square, MK 40 1SQ, were born.

Our own NIGERIAN BABIES with huge oil wells and gas fields near their huts eat only 1.5/day in our own NIGERIA, our own Mediocre, Wonky, Pure White Hereditary Racist, unashamedly functionally semi-illiterate, poly-educated poor man's son, a mere former debt-collector Solicitor in Norfolk/Norwich (5th Rate Partner), and the Senior Vice President of the Association of Her Majesty's District Judges, Bedford's District Judge Paul Robert Ayers, 3, St Paul's Square, MK 40 1SQ, a very, very, very, bellyful opportunist RACIST PURE WHITE BASTARD whose pure white father and mother have never seen CRUDE OIL, and whose pure white ancestors, John Foster (1759–1832), George Sharpe (?–1853). Robert Hibbert (1769–1849) Etcetera, were fed like battery hens with yields of millions of stolen children of defenceless poor people, including the pure black African ancestors of our IMPURE DUCHESS OF SUSSEX, Princess Ada Mazi Omu of Arochukwu, Princess Meghan Markle (43% Nigerian), and her impure children (<43% Nigerian)—**Habakkuk.**

Facts are sacred and cannot be overstated.

OYINBO OLE/ODE: They don't want their own MENTALLY GENTLER WHITE CHILDREN (OECD) and the pure white imbeciles they shepherd to know the TRUTH, which is that apart from our INFERIOR SKIN COLOUR and our Foreign Accent of speaking a Foreign Language, our own people (AFRICANS) are also properly created by Almighty God, so to conceal this TRUTH, and to save face, hereditary RACIST pure white bastards (predominantly but not exclusively pure white), CRIMINALLY steal yields of our own people's

(AFRICANS) Christ-granted talents, secure in the knowledge that all Judges would be PURE WHITE, and their hope is that they would be hereditary RACIST pure white bastards too—**Habakkuk 1:4.**

OXFORD, ENGLAND: GDC, Crooked, Hereditary Racist, Pure White Cougar, Mrs Helen Falcon (MBE), a ROTARIAN (a vulgarly charitable, hereditary white supremacist, and Antichrist Freemasonry without voodoo or occultists' ritual) unrelentingly lied under oath and on record—**Habakkuk 1:4.** The poor pure white ancestors of her pure white mother and father were incompetent RACIST LIARS too, like the ancestors of King's School and Oxbridge-educated Lord Justice Charles Anthony Haddon Cave, KC, a RACIST son of a very, very, very, rich Tasmanian Colonialist Economic Cannibal (**Mark 10:25**), an impostor and an expert of deception (perception is grander than reality), and a hereditary white supremacist descendant of DRUG LORDS (opium merchants of the Qing Dynasty), and a homie of Eton and Oxbridge-educated RICH MEN'S SON, Archbishop Justin Welby (**Mark 10:25**), they were THIEVES and owners of stolen children of defenceless poor people, including the pure black African ancestors of our IMPURE DUCHESS OF SUSSEX, Princess Ada Mazi Omu of Arochukwu, Princess Meghan Markle (43% Nigerian), and her impure children (<43% Nigerian)—**Habakkuk.**

OYINBO OLE/ODE: A very, very, very, DISHONEST typical pure white Englishwoman. A crooked closeted hereditary RACIST Member of the Most Excellent Order of our Empire of Stolen Inheritance—**Exodus 20:15.**

"The English think incompetence is the same thing as sincerity." Quentin Crisp (1908–1999).

BEDFORD, ENGLAND: Our own Mediocre, Wonky, Pure White Hereditary Racist, unashamedly functionally semi-illiterate, poly-educated poor man's son, a mere former debt-collector Solicitor in Norfolk/Norwich (5th Rate Partner), and the Senior Vice President of the Association of Her Majesty's District Judges, Bedford's District Judge Paul Robert Ayers, 3, St Paul's Square, MK 40 1SQ, you are a functional semi-illiterate. The land on which you were born yields only FOOD. You are rich. It is plainly deductible that the pure white ancestors of your own pure white father and mother were THIEVES and owners of stolen children of defenceless poor people, including the pure black African ancestors of our IMPURE DUCHESS OF SUSSEX, Princess Ada Mazi Omu of Arochukwu, Princess Meghan Markle (43% Nigerian), and her impure children (<43% Nigerian)—**Habakkuk.**

"Sometimes people don't want to hear the truth because they don't want their illusions destroyed." Friedrich Nietzsche (1844–1900).

TRUTHS disfavour hereditary RACIST pure white bastards (predominantly but not exclusively PURE WHITE). They have POWER and/or know those who have POWER. They use STOLEN AND/OR INHERITED POWER to subjugate TRUTHS. Skin colour that the very, very, very, fortunate wearer neither made nor chose is universally acknowledged to be IRREFUTABLY SUPERIOR, but the intellects are not, and their unashamedly MEDIOCRE Fish and Chips Justice System is fundamentally designed to subjugate TRUTHS—**Habakkuk 1:4.**

"Find the truth and tell it." Harold Pinter (1930–2008).

OYINBO OLE/ODE: Abuse of temporary power is the fullest definition of evil.

"Those who have the power to do wrong with impunity seldom wait long for the will." Dr Samuel Johnson (1709–1784).

Lord Leon Brittan (1939-2015): "A German Jew." Lord Denning (1899-1999).

FIVE: WOLLASTON, ENGLAND: GDC, Crooked, Hereditary Racist, and Pure White Rachael Bishop, England's Class Senior NHS Nurse, Northamptonshire, unrelentingly lied under oath and on record—**Habakkuk 1:4.** The poor pure white ancestors of her pure white mother and father were incompetent RACIST LIARS too, like the ancestors of King's School and Oxbridge-educated Lord Justice Charles Anthony Haddon Cave, KC, a RACIST son of a very, very, very, rich Tasmanian Colonialist Economic Cannibal (**Mark 10:25**), an impostor and an expert of deception (perception is grander than reality), and a hereditary white supremacist descendant of DRUG LORDS (opium merchants of the Qing Dynasty), and a homie of Eton and Oxbridge-educated RICH MEN'S SON, Archbishop Justin Welby (**Mark 10:25**), they were THIEVES and owners of stolen children of defenceless poor people, including the pure black African ancestors of our IMPURE DUCHESS OF SUSSEX, Princess Ada Mazi Omu of Arochukwu, Princess Meghan Markle (43% Nigerian), and her impure children (<43% Nigerian)—**Habakkuk.**

OYINBO OLE/ODE: A very, very, very, DISHONEST typical pure white Englishwoman. A crooked closeted hereditary RACIST Senior Nurse within one of the dullest adult populations in the industrialised world (OECD).

"A complaints such as Mrs Bishop's might trigger an enquiry." Pure White, Crooked, and Hereditary Racist Stephen Henderson, Head at MDDUS.

OYINBO OLE/ODE: Pure White, Crooked, and Hereditary Racist Stephen Henderson, dentist, Head at MDDUS, and our own Mediocre, Wonky, Pure White Hereditary Racist, unashamedly functionally semi-illiterate, poly-educated poor man's son, a mere former debt-collector Solicitor in

Norfolk/Norwich (5th Rate Partner), and the Senior Vice President of the Association of Her Majesty's District Judges, Bedford's District Judge Paul Robert Ayers, 3, St Paul's Square, MK 40 1SQ : Part of the resultant effects of several continuous centuries of STEALING and SLAVERY is that two very, very, very, bellyful PURE WHITE BASTARDS thrive in Great Britain.

Pure White, Crooked, and Hereditary Racist Stephen Henderson, Head at MDDUS, and Bedford's District Judge Paul Robert Ayers: Our own NIGERIAN BABIES with huge oil wells and gas fields near their huts eat only 1.5/day in our own NIGERIA, two very, very, very, bellyful pure white bastards whose pure white fathers and mothers have never seen CRUDE OIL, and whose pure white ancestors, including ultra-righteous John Bunyan (1628–1688), and the pure white ancestors of ANEURIN BEVAN (1897–1960) and DAME MARGARET SEWARD (1935–2021), were fed like battery hens with yields of millions of stolen children of defenceless poor people, including the pure Black African ancestors of the IMPURE (<43% Nigerian) great grandchildren of the DUKE OF EDINBURGH of blessed memory, Prince Phillip (1921–2021) thrive in Great Britain.

Philippians 1:21: Phillip was a 33rd Degree Freemason (Scottish Rite).

BEDFORD, ENGLAND: Our own Mediocre, Wonky, Pure White Hereditary Racist, unashamedly functionally semi-illiterate, poly-educated poor man's son, a mere former debt-collector Solicitor in Norfolk/Norwich (5th Rate Partner), and the Senior Vice President of the Association of Her Majesty's District Judges, Bedford's District Judge Paul Robert Ayers, 3, St Paul's Square, MK 40 1SQ, a brainless hereditary RACIST pure white bastard was granted the platform to display hereditary prejudice—**Habakkuk 1:4.**

MDDUS: Henderson: Letters: The Brain Isn't Skin Colour.

https://www.amazon.co.uk › MDDUS-Henderson-Letter…

Stephen Henderson's skin colour is indisputably superior; he neither made nor chose it. What else? An impostor. An expert of deception. PERCEPTION IS GRANDER …

OYINBO OLE/ODE. ACCURATE SEERS: They foresaw that Stephen Henderson will be a Head at MDDUS, and our own Mediocre, Wonky, Pure White Hereditary Racist, unashamedly functionally semi-illiterate, poly-educated poor man's son, a mere former debt-collector Solicitor in Norfolk/Norwich (5th Rate Partner), Bedford's District Judge Paul Robert Ayers, 3, St Paul's Square, MK 40 1SQ, will be our Senior Vice President of the Association of Her Majesty's District Judges, so they embarked on armed robbery and dispossession raids in AFRICA, and wherever they mercilessly slaughtered AFRICANS, they dispossessed them, and whenever they robbed AFRICANS, they took possession, and they used huge yields of several continuous centuries of merciless RACIST EVIL , the greediest economic cannibalism and the evilest RACIST TERRORISM the world will ever know—to create a very, very, very, LAVISH Socialist Eldorado for imbeciles, and decommissioned natural selection, and reversed progressive evolution, and made it possible for millions of pure white imbeciles to retrogressively breed more millions of pure white imbeciles (predominantly but not exclusively pure white).

Our own Mediocre, Wonky, Pure White Hereditary Racist, unashamedly functionally semi-illiterate, poly-educated poor man's son, a mere former debt-collector Solicitor in Norfolk/Norwich (5th Rate Partner), and the Senior Vice President of the Association of Her Majesty's District Judges, Bedford's District Judge Paul Robert Ayers, 3, St Paul's Square, MK 40 1SQ, our own MONEY, Nigeria (oil/gas) is by far more relevant to the economic survival of all your own mentally gentler white children, your own pure white mother, your pure white father, and your pure white spouse than bland and colourless Freemasons' KEMPSTON.

OYINBO OLE/ODE: Our own Mediocre, Wonky, Pure White Hereditary Racist, unashamedly functionally semi-illiterate, poly-educated poor man's son, a mere former debt-collector Solicitor in Norfolk/Norwich (5th Rate Partner), and the Senior Vice President of the Association of Her Majesty's District Judges, Bedford's District Judge Paul Robert Ayers, 3, St Paul's Square, MK 40 1SQ, an opportunist RACIST pure white bastard was granted the platform to display hereditary prejudice—**Habakkuk 1:4.** The only evidence of his very, very, very, HIGH IQ is the huge stolen inheritance that his thoroughly wretched pure white ancestors crossed the English Channel, not that long ago, without luggage or decent shoes to latch onto— **Habakkuk.**

Matthew 2:16: Hereditary RACIST pure white bastards (predominantly but not exclusively pure white): Anything the EVIL RACIST BASTARDS can't control, they destroy—**Matthew 14.**

Matthew 14: King's School and Oxbridge-educated Lord Justice Charles Anthony Haddon-Cave, KC, a RACIST son of a very, very RICH Tasmanian Colonialist Economic Cannibal(**Mark 10:25),** an ultra-righteous descendant of THIEVES, Opium Merchants, and owners of stolen children defenceless poor people, including the pure black African ancestors of our IMPURE DUCHESS OF SUSSEX, Princess Ada Mazi Omu of Arochukwu, Princess Meghan Markle (43% Nigerian), and her impure children (<43% Nigerian)—**Habakkuk**, was John jailed because he lied, or did the intolerant LUNATIC JEW remove his head because he was MENTAL?

Matthew 27: 32–56: King's School and Oxbridge-educated Lord Justice Charles Anthony Haddon-Cave, KC, a RACIST son of a very, very RICH Tasmanian Colonialist Economic Cannibal(**Mark 10:25**), an ultra-righteous descendant of THIEVES, Opium Merchants, and owners of stolen children defenceless poor people, including the pure black African ancestors of our IMPURE DUCHESS OF SUSSEX, Princess Ada Mazi Omu of Arochukwu, Princess Meghan Markle (43% Nigerian), and her impure children (<43% Nigerian)—**Habakkuk**, was the fellow kidnapped and lynched like Gadhafi because He lied, or was He crucified because He was MENTAL?

A BRAINLESS HEREDITARY RACIST ONE-DIMENSIONALLY EDUCATED PURE WHITE BASTARD—**HABAKKUK 1:4**.

Bedford's District Judge Paul Robert Ayers, for your own unashamedly MEDIOCRE Fish and chips Justice System to work as designed, you must have SUPREME KNOWLEDGE, but you don't, as intellect has absolutely nothing to do with your universally acknowledged irrefutably SUPERIOR SKIN COLOUR, which you neither made nor chose, so you criminally destroy AFRICANS who know that they are a BRAINLESS PURE WHITE BASTARD—by criminally stealing yields of our own people's (AFRICANS) Christ-granted talents, and secure in the knowledge that all Judges would be pure white and they would be hereditary white supremacist bastards too. No brain. Poor natural resources. Several continuous centuries of stealing and SLAVERY preceded your huge stolen inheritance. Before SLAVERY, what?

"Affluence is not a birth right." Lord Cameron.

Facts are sacred and cannot be overstated: Bedford's District Judge Paul Robert Ayers, it is not the TRUTH that daily dialogues with PURE WHITE IMBECILES (predominantly but not exclusively pure white) is a proper job that is worthwhile and manly.

Proverbs 17:16: "They may not have been well written from a grammatical point of view but I am confident I had not forgotten any of the facts." Crooked, Hereditary Racist, and Pure White Welsh Bastard, Geraint Evans, England's Class Welsh Senior Postgraduate Tutor, Oxford.

Proverbs 17:16: "The best opportunity of developing academically and emotional." Bedford's District Judge Paul Robert Ayers.

OUR OWN RACIST MORON MASON OF OUR OWN EMPIRE OF STOLEN INHERITANCE - OYINBO OLE/ODE. BEFORE SLAVERY, WHAT - **HABAKKUK**?

Proverbs 17:16: Bedford's District Judge Paul Robert Ayers, our own brainless, intellectually ungifted, and poly-educated son of plebeian nobodies, a mere former debt collector Solicitor in bland and colourless Norwich (Lowlife 5th Rate Partner); if our ignorant opportunist RACIST pure white bastard, albeit England's Class Senior Judge, read his approved Judgement, he was a PURE WHITE RACIST FOOL, and if he did not, he lied as he implied that he did— **Habakkuk 1:4.** The very, very, very, poor pure white ancestors of his own pure white father and mother were incompetent RACIST LIARS too, like the very, very, very, rich pure white ancestors of King's School and Oxbridge-educated Lord Justice Charles Anthony Haddon-Cave, KC, a RACIST son of a Colonialist Economic Cannibal (**Mark 10:25**), Oxbridge-educated rich man's son, Sir Charles Phillip Haddon-Cave (1925–1999), an impostor and an expert of deception (perception is grander than reality), and a closeted white supremacist descendant of DRUG LORDS (opium merchants of the Qing Dynasty), and a homie of Eton and Oxbridge-educated very, very, very, rich men's son, Archbishop Justin Welby (**Mark 10:25**), they were THIEVES and owners of stolen children of defenceless poor people, including the pure black African ancestors of our IMPURE DUCHESS OF SUSSEX, Princess Ada Mazi Omu of Arochukwu, Princess Meghan Markle (43% Nigerian), and her impure children (<43% Nigerian)—**Habakkuk**.

OYINBO OLE/ODE: Then, they carried and sold millions of stolen children of defenceless poor people, including the pure black African ancestors of our IMPURE DUCHESS OF SUSSEX, Princess Ada Mazi Omu of Arochukwu, Princess Meghan Markle (43% Nigerian), and her impure children (<43% Nigerian)—**Habakkuk**, now THIEVES steal our own natural resources from our own AFRICA - **Habakkuk.** It is not the truth that our true chains are off.

Only our visible chains are removed, our true chains will never be voluntarily removed. Only very, very, very, STUPID AFRICANS expect others to voluntarily relinquish several centuries-old advantageous positions in exchange for NOTHING; substitution is likely.

SUBSTITUTION IS FRAUDULENT EMANCIPATION - **HABAKKUK**.

"Moderation is a virtue only among those who are thought to have found alternatives." Dr Henry Kissinger (1923–2023).

OYINBO OLE/ODE: Our own Nigerian babies with huge oil wells and gas fields near their huts eat only 1.5/day in our own NIGERIA; two, only two, but two too many very, very, very, bellyful pure white bastards, Bedford's District Judge Paul Robert Ayers and Geraint Evans, England's Class Senior Postgraduate Tutor, Oxford, whose pure white fathers and mothers have never seen CRUDE OIL; unlike Putin's Russia, there are no oil wells or gas fields in bland and colourless Freemasons' Kempston and in the Valleys of Wales, including in Nick Griffin's Llanerfyl Powys, and hereditary white supremacist bastards whose pure white ancestors including the pure white ancestors of ANEURIN BEVAM (1897–1960) and DAME MARGARET SEWARD (1935–2021), were fed like battery hens with yields of millions of stolen children of defenceless poor people, including the pure Black African ancestors of the IMPURE (<43% Nigerian) great grandchildren of the Duke of Edinburgh of Blessed Memory, Prince Phillip (1921–2021)—thrive in Great Britain. Which part of our own shithole Africa is great?

Philippians 1:21: Phillip was a 33rd Degree Freemason (Scottish Rite).

Then, all Judges were pure white Freemasons, and most of them were thicker than a gross of planks.

Bedford's District Judge Paul Robert Ayers, a brainless hereditary RACIST pure white bastard DISHONESTLY implied that he did not know that SLAVERY rebuilt everything it succeeded and paid for everything it preceded, including Aneurin Bevan's NHS (1948), Dame Margaret Seward's GDC (1956), Bedford County Court, MK40 1SQ (preceded by Slavery), and Bedfordshire Masonic Centre, MK42 8AH (preceded by Slavery). Equitable, fair, and just REPARATION pends, and several centuries of unpaid interest accrue – **Habakkuk.**

"Britain's justice system is racist and should not be trusted by ethnic minorities." Peter Herbert, OBE.

Luke 11:52: Future Sir Peter Herbert, KBE, an expert of their law, there is no new news in your news, so kindly expatiate. Is it legal to KILL verifiably crooked hereditary white supremacist Freemason Judges—**Exodus 21:23–27**, or what?

Future Sir Peter Herbert, KBE, an expert of their law (**Luke 11:52**), what must we do to balance the unbalanced? **Matthew 14:** Should persecuted AFRICANS resort to Kamikaze and remove the heads of crooked white supremacist Judges?

"Give us the tools, and we shall finish the job." Sir Winston Churchill (1874-1965).

Your Majesty, the Defender of our own faith - **John 14:6**, give us the nod, and we shall 'KILL' the New Pharisees, crooked experts of their law (**Luke 11:52**); crooked hereditary white supremacist bastard Freemason Judges – **Habakkuk 1:4.**

"Sir, you are to consider that in our constitution, according to its true principles, the King is the head, he is supreme: he is above everything, and there is no power by which he can be tried. Therefore, it is, Sir, that we hold the King can do no wrong; that whatever may happen to be wrong in government may not be above our reach, by being ascribed to Majesty. Redress is always to be had against oppression, by punishing the immediate agents. The King, though he should command, cannot force a Judge to condemn a man unjustly; therefore, it is the Judge whom we prosecute and punish. Political institutions are formed upon the consideration of what will frequently tend to the good of the whole, although now and then exceptions may occur. Thus, it is better in general that a nation should have a supreme legislative power, although it may at times be abused. And then, Sir, there is this consideration, that if the abuse is numerous, Nature will rise, and claiming her original rights, overturn a corrupt political system." Dr Samuel Johnson (1709–1784).

BEDFORD, ENGLAND: District Judge Paul Robert Ayers, a brainless hereditary RACIST pure white bastard was granted the platform to display hereditary prejudice; let me tell you, there, we will be armed, and we shall stand our ground against any mother fu*ker. The most important part of the matter is MONEY, and it is not the yield of your talent or land. You are rich only because your ancestors were THIEVES (**Exodus 20:15**), extremely nasty and merciless RACIST MURDERERS (**Exodus 20:13**), and owners of stolen children of defenceless poor people, including the pure black African ancestors of our IMPURE DUCHESS OF SUSSEX, Princess Ada Mazi Omu of Arochukwu, Princess Meghan Markle (43% Nigerian), and her impure children (<43% Nigerian)—**Habakkuk**. You should stay here, it is safer. There, we shall find you, or pay people to find you, and we shall take revenge, albeit only LEGALLY, under God's Law—**Exodus 21:23–27.**

Dr Mungo Park (1771-1806) had guns. Then, he was killed, now his type would be kidnapped and exchanged for ransom: Great Britain is the sixth largest economy on earth.

"We shall deal with the racist bastards when we get out of prison." Comrade Robert Mugabe (1924-2019).

Facts are sacred and they cannot be overstated: "The truth allows no choice." Dr Samuel Johnson (1709–1784).

OYINBO OLE/ODE: PERCEPTION IS GRANDER THAN REALITY. EVERYTHING, ABSOLUTELY EVERYTHING IS BRAINLESSLY AND BASELESSLY ASSUMED IN FAVOUR OF THE UNIVERSALLY ACKNOWLEDGED IRREFUTABLY SUPERIOR SKIN COLOUR THAT THE VERY, VERY, VERY, FORTUNATE WEARER NEITHER MADE NOR CHOSE—**HABAKKUK.**

Proverbs 20:15: Skin colour is a great creation of Almighty God, but it is not the greatest: OYINBO OLE/ODE.

BEDFORD, ENGLAND: District Judge Paul Robert Ayers, let me tell you the TRUTH, and I stake my life on it, our own MONEY, our own NIGERIA, is Shell's docile cash cow since 1956 (Oloibiri). GDC was established in 1956. Unlike PUTIN'S RUSSIA, there are no oil wells or gas fields in bland and colourless NORFOLK/NORWICH (Coastal Dole/the Departure Lounge of Life) and where your own pure white father and mother were born: OYINBO OLE/ODE - **Habakkuk.**

BEDFORD, ENGLAND: District Judge Paul Robert Ayers, let me tell you, based on very, very, very, proximate observations and direct experiences, you have all the characteristics of an impudent Scottish Leech. You are not a SAINT because the pure white ancestors of your pure white father and mother were THIEVES and owners of stolen children of defenceless poor people, including the pure black African ancestors of our IMPURE DUCHESS OF SUSSEX, Princess Ada Mazi Omu of Arochukwu, Princess Meghan Markle (43% Nigerian), and her impure children (<43% Nigerian)—**Habakkuk.**

OYINBO OLE/ODE: 'The impudence of an Irishman is the impudence of a fly, that buzzes about you, and you put it away, but it returns and flutters and teases you. The impudence of a Scotsman is the impudence of a leech, that fixes and sucks your blood.' Dr Samuel Johnson (1709–1784).

Their people are everywhere, and they control almost everything, including RACIAL HATRED and FRAUD. Integrity, friendship, respect, and charity: All for one, and for all.

BEDFORD, ENGLAND: District Judge Paul Robert Ayers, let me tell you, Slavery is different from Colonisation, and Colonisation is different from Neo-Colonialism, but they are all variants of RACIST ECONOMIC CANNIBALISM—**Habakkuk.**

Exodus 20:15: They will forever, till Thy Kingdom Come, steal from AFRICA. What very, very, very, greedy bastards steal from AFRICA will vary and will depend on what insatiably greedy bastards need. Then, they carried and sold millions of stolen children of defenceless poor people, including the pure black African ancestors of our IMPURE DUCHESS OF SUSSEX, Princess Ada Mazi Omu of Arochukwu, Princess Meghan Markle (43% Nigerian), and her impure children (<43% Nigerian)—**Habakkuk**, now THIEVES steal our own natural resources from our own AFRICA.

"How Europe underdeveloped Africa." Dr Walter Rodney (1942–1980).

"Jews are very good with money." President Trump

"Jews are intelligent and creative, Chinese are intelligent but not creative, Indians are servile, and Africans are morons." Prof James Watson (DNA) paraphrased.

"Trump's administration packed courts with white Judges." Kamala Harris

Luke 11:52: Based on several decades of very, very, very, proximate observations and direct experiences, homogeneity in the administration of their law is the impregnable secure mask of MERCILESS RACIST EVIL, an intelligently designed weapon of RACE WAR—**Habakkuk 1:4.**

John 5:22: God Almighty Judges no one. Then, very, very, very, greedy crooked bastards won in crooked courts before crooked Judges, but in the WAR when the Corporal flipped, the only SINLESS JUDGE looked away (**Matthew 25:31–46**), and insatiably greedy bastards lost everything and more. If they were GENIUSES, as they seemed to brag, why didn't they foresee that the Corporal would flip, and why didn't self-awarded God's favourites help themselves when he did?

Proverbs 20:15: Ignorance is bliss: "Those whose who know the least obey the best." George Farquhar (1677–1707).

GOOGLE: BIAFRIA MARK II.

PURE WHITE BRITISH SOLDIER (TERRITORIAL DEFENCE): GDC, Crooked, Hereditary Racist, and Pure White Bastard, Stephanie Twidale (TD) unrelentingly lied under oath and on record—**Habakkuk 1:4**. The poor pure white ancestors of her pure white father and mother were incompetent RACIST LIARS too, like the pure white ancestors of King's School and Oxbridge-educated Lord Justice Charles Anthony Haddon Cave, KC, a RACIST son of a very, very, very, rich Colonialist Economic Cannibal, an impostor and an expert of deception (perception is grander than reality), and a hereditary white supremacist descendant of DRUG LORDS (opium merchants of the Qing Dynasty), a homie of Eton and Oxbridge-educated very, very, very, RICH MEN'S SON, Archbishop Justin Welby, they were THIEVES and owners of stolen children of defenceless poor people, including the pure black African ancestors of our IMPURE DUCHESS OF SUSSEX, Princess Ada Mazi Omu of Arochukwu, Princess Meghan Markle (43% Nigerian), and her impure children (<43% Nigerian)—**Habakkuk.**

A very, very, very, DISHONEST typical pure white Englishwoman. A crooked closeted hereditary RACIST British soldier – **Habakkuk 1:4.**

GDC: Had the Crooked, Hereditary Racist Pure White Bastard, Stephanie Twidale (TD), England's Class British Soldier, albeit our TERRITORIAL DEFENDER, had she been as impure as impure MEGHAN MARKLE (43% Nigerian), the hereditary RACIST pure white bastard would have been in a BIG TROUBLE. Her type killed the INDIAN, only 42, and the NIGERIAN, only 56, albeit hand's off, with the mens rea in the belly of the actus.

Google: Dr Richard Bamgboye, GP.

Google: Dr Anand Kamath, Dentist.

Exodus 21:23–27: Stephanie Twidale (TD), our crooked hereditary RACIST pure white bastards British Soldier (TD) should stay here, it is safer: There, we shall take revenge, one tooth for one tooth, and one life for only one life.

John 14:26: When the Divine unraveller of MERCILESS RACIST EVIL unravels UNCONTROLLABLE HERDITARY RACIAL HATRED, to save face, crooked hereditary RACIST pure white bastards unleash their EVIL RACIST THUNDER, the Lunatic Negro Card: Any Negro who disagrees with any member of their brainlessly and baselessly self-awarded SUPERIOR RACE is a mad man with a stick in his hand, so opportunist RACIST pure white bastards knock down our own people (AFRICANS).

"If a madman were to come into this room with a stick in his hand, no doubt we should pity the state of his mind; but our primary consideration would be to take care of ourselves. We should knock him down first, and pity him afterwards." Dr Samuel Johnson (1709–1784).

ARCHIE IS IMPURE, <43% NIGERIAN. BEDFORD, ENGLAND: Bedford's District Judge Paul Robert, why are you pure (100% white)?

A Racist descendant of ECONOMIC MIGRANTS from Eastern Europe—with an arbitrarily acquired camouflage English name. He looked physically ill-favoured and mentally wonky. Had he been as BLACK as 'UGLY' former Judge Constance Briscoe, and thrice as smart, the opportunist RACIST pure white bastard wouldn't be the Senior Vice President of the Association of Her Majesty's District Judges – **Habakkuk 1:4.**

Psalm 116:11: It is not the TRUTH that 'UGLY', Negress, former Judge Constance Briscoe, was the only incompetently dishonest Judge in Great Britain.

Google: The White Judge Lied.

"Lies are told all the time." Sir Mr Justice Robert Michael Havers (1923–1992), QC,

American and Russian Soldiers amicably camped side by side near NIGER'S URANIUM, our own Mediocre, Wonky, Pure White Hereditary Racist, unashamedly functionally semi-illiterate, poly-educated poor man's son, a mere former debt-collector Solicitor in Norfolk/Norwich (5th Rate Partner), and the Senior Vice President of the Association of Her Majesty's District Judges, Bedford's District Judge Paul Robert Ayers, 3, St Paul's Square, MK 40 1SQ, a RACIST semi-illiterate pure white bastard, alleged 33rd Degree Freemason, and descendant of Slaves and Opium Merchants, whose pure white mother and father might not know the ATOMIC NUMBER OF URANIUM was our Senior Judge.

BEDFORD,ENGLAND: Our own Mediocre, Wonky, Pure White Hereditary Racist, unashamedly functionally semi-illiterate, poly-educated poor man's son, a mere former debt-collector Solicitor in Norfolk/Norwich (5th Rate Partner), and the Senior Vice President of the Association of Her Majesty's District Judges, Bedford's District Judge Paul

Robert Ayers, 3, St Paul's Square, MK 40 1SQ, why is England very, very, very, RICH, the sixth largest economy on earth? Is the HUGE WEALTH the yield of your talent, or is it the yield of the very, very, very, HIGH IQs of your own pure white mother and father: OYINBO OLE/ODE?

QUASI-COMMUNISM: HEREDITARY RACIST PURE WHITE BASTARDS ARTIFICIALLY CREATED FAKE JOBS FOR CROOKED HEREDITARY RACIST PURE WHITE BASTARDS (PREDOMINANTLY BUT NOT EXCLUSIVELY PURE WHITE), TO THE DETRIMENT OF FOREIGNERS—**LEVITICUS 19:33–34.**

****

GDC CHAMBERS, 20.11.2008: DAVID MORRIS (BARRISTER THAT WAS INSTRUCTED BY THE MPS): Again, from Sue Gregory in August 2006 no, sorry, John Hooper 2006. John Hooper is another colleague at Bedford, is that correct?

CHARLOTTE DOWLING GOODSON (NHS): That's correct; he was one of the managers in my team

DAVID MORRIS (BARRISTER THAT WAS INSTRUCTED BY THE MPS): Referring to, 'Stephanie Twidale calling us a few weeks ago and she wanted to know if there had been a dental inspection there at all (I think that's Bedfordshire) and I didn't know the answer. Cue Richard, have you carried out an inspection at this practice. Please could you advise Stephanie when she contacts you'. That is the next time this matter arose, is that right?

CHARLOTTE DOWLING GOODSON (NHS): That is correct, yes.

DAVID MORRIS (BARRISTER THAT WAS INSTRUCTED BY THE MPS): And then I think in response to that, do we get an e mail from Richard Hill, which we have behind tab 21 in volume 1.

CHARLOTTE DOWLING GOODSON (NHS): Sorry, can I have the tab again.

DAVID MORRIS (BARRISTER THAT WAS INSTRUCTED BY THE MPS): Tab 21. From Richard Hill 6 September 06 to you and others at Bedford; record of practice visits, and we have the entry on that schedule for July 2004, all right?

CHARLOTTE DOWLING GOODSON (NHS): Yes.

DAVID MORRIS (BARRISTER THAT WAS INSTRUCTED BY THE MPS): And did you, as part of his process then well, I can see the concerns that were raised in that column: no risk assessment, no COSSH, Kavoclave type autoclave, why that shouldn't be used, no other members of practice staff present at visits, and could not be questioned regarding cross infection control by the practice. But did you, as part of this process, receive a copy of what was purported to be the visit record for that date 22 July 04?

CHARLOTTE DOWLING GOODSON (NHS): Not at that time, but we did get copies of the reports and for these visits at a later date. We had been requesting them.

DAVID MORRIS (BARRISTER THAT WAS INSTRUCTED BY THE MPS): That is D5, if you can have a look at that, please. [Handed]

CHARLOTTE DOWLING GOODSON (NHS): Thank you (Perused document).

DAVID MORRIS (BARRISTER THAT WAS INSTRUCTED BY THE MPS): And I think if I can take you to the feedback, final page, page 5, summary of these concerns: 'The practice uses a Kavoclave type autoclave.

This is not acceptable. There is also a large turnover of staff and I am not satisfied that staff training is at an acceptable level and have concerns over the cross infection control procedures', and the essential action points set out there. So you would have received that, and that would have informed your concerns at that time about that practice?

CHARLOTTE DOWLING GOODSON (NHS): This report was received at a later time. I did not receive it until 2004

DAVID MORRIS (BARRISTER THAT WAS INSTRUCTED BY THE MPS): No.

CHARLOTTE DOWLING GOODSON (NHS): But what I also I received was part of the decision making process, and prioritising the practice for an inspection by the DRS.
DAVID MORRIS (BARRISTER THAT WAS INSTRUCTED BY THE MPS): And would those concerns, informed in part by that report, have been fed through to Stephanie Twidale prior to her conducting her inspection in February 07?

CHARLOTTE DOWLING GOODSON (NHS): I can't remember if I passed them on. I think Richard Hill would have shared those issues with Stephanie as part of the discussion prior to the visit, and that is part of the reason why Richard went with Stephanie to undertake the visit with her.

DAVID MORRIS (BARRISTER THAT WAS INSTRUCTED BY THE MPS): It would have made a lot of sense for the information in that report to have been passed on and fed through as necessary preliminary material prior to inspection?

CHARLOTTE DOWLING GOODSON (NHS): Yes, it would have been. DAVID MORRIS (BARRISTER THAT WAS INSTRUCTED BY THE MPS): And do you appreciate that now, very recently, Mr. Hill has realised that that report, relating to Mr. Bamgbelu's practice, in fact was an error, in as much as the concerns in it related to wholly different matters?

CHARLOTTE DOWLING GOODSON (NHS): No, I was not aware of that.

***

'Not at that time, but we did get copies of the reports and for these visits at a later date. We had been requesting them.' Charlotte Dowling Goodson (NHS), under oath, 20.11.2008.

NEGRO'S PERSPECTIVE:

Psalm 144: They tell incompetent racist lies all the time, but they lie that they don't lie.

Psalm 116:11: "Lies are told all the time." Oxbridge-educated very, very, very, rich man's son (Mark 10:25), Sir Mr Justice Robert Michael Havers (1923-1992), QC.

Our own Mediocre, Wonky, Pure White Hereditary Racist, unashamedly functionally semi-illiterate, poly-educated poor man's son, a mere former debt-collector Solicitor in Norfolk/Norwich (5th Rate Partner), and the Senior Vice President of the Association of Her Majesty's District Judges, Bedford's District Judge Paul Robert Ayers, 3, St Paul's Square, MK 40 1SQ, based on very, very, very, proximate observations and direct experiences, you have all the characteristics of an IMPUDENT SCOTTISH LEECH, and the pure ancestors of your pure white mother and father were THIEVES: Extremely nasty and merciless RACIST MURDERERS, nastier than Yevgeny Prigozhin (1961–2023) and Hitler (1889–1945): Several years of NAZI HOLOCAUST (1939–1945) were a mee storm in a teacup in comparison to several continuous centuries of MAAFA

(1445–1888), and they were industrial-scale professional armed robbers, armed land grabbers, GUN RUNNERS, Opium Merchants of the Qing Dynasty). and owners of stolen children of defenceless poor people, including the pure black African ancestors of our IMPURE DUCHESS OF SUSSEX, Princess Ada Mazi Omu of Arochukwu, Princess Meghan Markle (43% Nigerian), and her impure children (<43% Nigerian)—**Habakkuk.**

OYINBO OLE/ODE: BEDFORD'S DISTRICT JUDGE PAUL ROBERT AYERS, ENGLAND'S CLASS SENIOR JUDGE. AN IGNORANT HEREDITARY RACIST DESCENDANT OF ULTRA-RIGHTEOUS PURE WHITE PROFESSIONAL THIEVES AND OWNERS OF STOLEN CHILDREN OF DEFENCELESS POOR PEOPLE (AFRICANS) HAS A GROSSLY EXAGGERATED SENSE OF SELF-WORTH— **HABAKKUK.**

BEDFORD, ENGLAND: GDC. Pure White, Crooked, and Hereditary Racist Sue Gregory (OBE) unrelentingly lied under implied oath and on record—**Habakkuk 1:4.** The poor pure white ancestors of her pure white father and mother were incompetent RACIST LIARS too, like the pure white ancestors of King's School and Oxbridge-educated Lord Justice Charles Anthony Haddon-Cave, KC, a RACIST son of a very, very, very, RICH Tasmanian Colonialist Economic Cannibal (**Mark 10:25),** Sir Charles Phillip Haddon-Cave (1925–1999), a properly schooled impostor and an expert of deception, and a closeted hereditary white supremacist descendant of DRUG LORDS (Opium Merchants of the Qing Dynasty), and a homie of Eton and Oxbridge-educated rich men's son (**Mark 10:25**), Archbishop Justin Welby, they were THIEVES and owners of stolen children of defenceless poor people, including the pure black African ancestors of our IMPURE DUCHESS OF SUSSEX, Princess Ada Mazi Omu of Arochukwu,

Princess Meghan Markle (43% Nigerian), and her impure children (<43% Nigerian)—**Habakkuk.**

"The English think incompetence is the same thing as sincerity." Quentin Crisp (1908–1999).

A very, very, very, dishonest typical pure white Englishwoman. A closeted hereditary RACIST Officer of the Most Excellent Order of our Empire of Stolen Inheritance—Habakkuk. Her type killed the NIGERIAN, only 56, and the INDIAN, only 42.

"He is a typical Englishman, usually violent and always dull." Wilde (1854–1900).

Only a pure white woman can beget a pure white child: The Duchess of Sussex is IMPURE (<43 Nigerian), so her children are impure Royals, <43% Nigerians.

Google: Dr Richard Bamgboye, GP.

Google: Dr Anand Kamath, Dentist.

Leviticus 19:33–34: They kill foreigners, only foreigners, albeit hands-off, with the mens rea hidden in the belly of the actus reus—**Exodus 20:13.**

Exodus 21: 23–27: They should fu*king stay here, it is safer. There, we shall take revenge, a tooth for a tooth.

"You will bow. You can't beat the system." Our Born-Again Christian

Exodus 20:5: I shan't, and I am prepared to perish in the process.

1 John 4:4, John 14:6, Romans 11: I know who will.

Mark 10:25: Elon Musk: Hereditary Intra-Racial Sex Machine.

SIX: She prays to CHRIST and pays TITHE (Quasi-Protection Money) at Church Minister, John Foster's Brickhill, and Mediocre Mafia (Freemasons) in KEMPSTON answer all her prayers.

EKITI OLE: TWO MEAL TICKETS: 2 **THESSALONIANS 3:6–10:**

Which of one of our PUTRID TUBES did our Born-Again Christian tell our own Mediocre, Wonky, Pure White Hereditary Racist, unashamedly functionally semi-illiterate, poly-educated poor man's son, a mere former debt-collector Solicitor in Norfolk/Norwich (5th Rate Partner), and the Senior Vice President of the Association of Her Majesty's District Judges, Bedford's District Judge Paul Robert Ayers, 3, St Paul's Square, MK 40 1SQ and Freemasons at Brickhill Baptist Church, and in Kempston (the Keep), she used to work for 0.5M? Our own glorified hoe.

"I emphasis the point." Our own Mediocre, Wonky, Pure White Hereditary Racist, unashamedly functionally semi-illiterate, poly-educated poor man's son, a mere former debt-collector Solicitor in Norfolk/Norwich (5th Rate Partner), and the Senior Vice President of the Association of Her Majesty's District Judges, Bedford's District Judge Paul Robert Ayers, 3, St Paul's Square, MK 40 1SQ.

OYINBO OLODO/OYINBO ODE: A brainless hereditary RACIST pure white bastard was granted the platform to display hereditary prejudice: If he read his approved Judgement, he was a FOOL, and if he did not, he lied as he implied that he did—**Habakkuk 1:4.**

Facts are sacred and cannot be overstated.

In our own NIGERIA, a properly proof-read and approved Judgement by our own NIGERIAN JUDGE, must pass through at least four separate filters: The transcript writers, the Proof-readers, the Court Clerks, and the Judge.

In an open dialogue with Justice Ruth Bader Ginsburg (1933–2020), Lady Hale lamented funding.

My Lady, what is the value of unashamed mediocrity and confusion?

TRUMP'S POODLES: FLAT TRACK BULLIES.

GOOGLE: IMAGBON,1892.

"Ethical Foreign Policy." Robin Cook (1946–2005)

Their hairs stand on end when they are challenged by AFRICANS, we and our type are the ones RACIST BASTARDS would beat up without the support of the YANKS.

The Keep (Territorial Defence) Bedford Road, Kempston, MK42 8AH. **Psalm 118:22, Luke 20:17**: If the BUILDERS are as ethical and as brave as they brag, the hereditary white supremacist bastards should use overwhelming extreme violence to evict PUTIN from CRIMEA, he used extreme overwhelming violence to convert Bakhmut from bricks to rubble and stole it—**Exodus 20:15.**

Habakkuk 1:4: Then, all Judges were pure white Freemasons, and most of them were THICKER than a gross of planks, and they sent their daughters—too, to universities, to gain qualifications, so that they can eat their own food (**2 Thessalonians 3:6-10**), but also to use their PUTRID TUBES to ensnare fellow university students, their SECOND MEAL TICKET—Quasi-hoes.

If King's School and Oxbridge-educated, Lord Justice Charles Anthony Haddon-Cave, KC, a RACIST son of a very, very, very, rich Tasmanian Colonialist Economic Cannibal (**Mark 10:25**), an impostor and an expert of deception (perception is grander than reality), and a hereditary white supremacist descendant of DRUG LORDS (opium merchants of the Qing Dynasty), and a homie of Eton and Oxbridge-educated very, very, very, very, rich men's son, Archbishop Justin Welby (**Mark 10:25**), could disprove the TRUTH, which is that Sue Gregory (OBE), Officer of the Most Excellent Order of our own Empire of STOLEN INHERITANCE, unrelentingly lied under implied oath and on record, he will confirm the belief of lots and lots of his own pure white kindred, which is that that Peter Herbert (OBE) lied when he implied that the administration of English Law is crooked and indiscreetly RACIST and should not be trusted by NEGROES—**Habakkuk 1:4.**

House of Commons—Constitutional Affairs—First Report

https://publications.parliament.uk › cmselect › cmconst

He actively encouraged ethnic minority applications, agreeing to look personally into the grievances of any applicant [and] the Society is aware of a number of …

"England: About Thirty Million, Mostly Fools." Thomas Carlyle (1795–1881).

1880: The Royal College of Surgeons

1881: Thomas Carlyle and Benjamin Disraeli died.

1882: The Royal Courts of Justice

1884: Scramble for Africa: The Partitioning of Africa by very, very, very, greedy European economic cannibals.

Unearned patronages, and undeserved privileges: King's School and Oxbridge-educated, Lord Justice Charles Anthony Haddon-Cave, KC, a RACIST son of a very, very, very, rich Tasmanian Colonialist Economic Cannibal (**Mark 10:25**), and a hereditary white supremacist descendant of DRUG LORDS (opium merchants of the

Qing Dynasty), and a homie of Eton and Oxbridge-educated very, very, very, very, rich men's son, Archbishop Justin Welby **(Mark 10:25),** which part of the Royal Courts of Justice (1882), WC2A 2LL, was not STOLEN, or which part did your own pure white father, Sir Charles Phillip Haddon-Cave (1925–1999) buy, or which part preceded SLAVERY: The very, very,. very, impressive building, or its very, very, very, expensive chattels?

King's School and Oxbridge-educated, Lord Justice Charles Anthony Haddon-Cave, KC, a RACIST son of a very, very, very, rich Tasmanian Colonialist Economic Cannibal **(Mark 10:25)**, an impostor and an expert of deception (perception is grander than reality), and and a hereditary white supremacist descendant of DRUG LORDS (opium merchants of the Qing Dynasty), and a homie of Eton and Oxbridge-educated very, very, very, very, rich men's son, Archbishop Justin Welby **(Mark 10:25),** a brainless hereditary RACIST pure white bastard dishonestly implied that he did not know that his own pure white ancestors were THIEVES and owners of stolen children of defenceless poor people, including the pure black African ancestors of our IMPURE DUCHESS OF SUSSEX, Princess Ada Mazi Omu of Arochukwu, Princess Meghan Markle (43% Nigerian), and her impure children (<43% Nigerian)— **Habakkuk**. He also lied when he dishonestly implied that he did not know that SLAVERY rebuilt everything it succeeded and paid for everything it preceded, including the Royal Courts of Justice (1882), NHS (1948), and GDC (1956).

"The blame is his who chooses. God is blameless." Plato

I am the product of my upbringing, so I am not responsible for it. King's School and Oxbridge-educated, Lord Justice Charles Anthony Haddon-Cave, KC, a RACIST son of a very, very, very, rich Tasmanian Colonialist Economic

Cannibal (**Mark 10:25**), an impostor and an expert of deception (perception is grander than reality), and a hereditary white supremacist descendant of DRUG LORDS (opium merchants of the Qing Dynasty), and a homie of Eton and Oxbridge-educated very, very, very, very, rich men's son, Archbishop Justin Welby (**Mark 10:25**), I was brought up to look down on you and your type, and I do. You are a LEECH, and your ancestors were THIEVES and owners of stolen children of defenceless poor people, including the pure black African ancestors of our IMPURE DUCHESS OF SUSSEX, Princess Ada Mazi Omu of Arochukwu, Princess Meghan Markle (43% Nigerian), and her impure children (<43% Nigerian)—**Habakkuk.**

Michael Portillo, Mohammed Al Fayed (1929–2023), Yinka Bamgbelu, and Ali Kemal (1867–1922) did not arbitrarily acquire camouflage English names, our own Mediocre, Wonky, Pure White Hereditary Racist, unashamedly functionally semi-illiterate, poly-educated poor man's son, a mere former debt-collector Solicitor in Norfolk/Norwich (5th Rate Partner), and the Senior Vice President of the Association of Her Majesty's District Judges, Bedford's District Judge Paul Robert Ayers, 3, St Paul's Square, MK 40 1SQ, what is the real name of your own father, where did he come from, and when? Or did your pure white ancestors evolve from MAMI WATA in the River Great Ouse? A brainless hereditary RACIST pure white bastard was granted the platform to display hereditary prejudice – **Habakkuk 1:4.**

BEDFORD, ENGLAND: Our own Mediocre, Wonky, Pure White Hereditary Racist, unashamedly functionally semi-illiterate, poly-educated poor man's son, a mere former debt-collector Solicitor in Norfolk/Norwich (5th Rate Partner), and the Senior Vice President of the Association of Her Majesty's District Judges, Bedford's District Judge Paul Robert Ayers, 3, St Paul's Square, MK 40 1SQ, only if he did, had your own pure white father not arbitrarily acquired a camouflage English name, you wouldn't have been our Senior Judge in BEDFORD, Great Britain. Which part of our own shithole Africa is great?

Had Ali Kemal (1867–1922) been as rich as Mohammed Al Fayed (1929–2023), Boris Johnson would have been Mohammed Ali, and he would not have been our PREMIER.

Saxe-Coburg, and Gotha family arbitrarily acquired a camouflage English name in 1917. Gustav Liebson (1876–1947), a Latvian Jew, arbitrarily acquired a camouflage English name in 1925; had he not, NIGEL LAWSON wouldn't have been our Chancellor.

Gigantic yields of millions of stolen children of defenceless poor people, including the pure black African ancestors of our IMPURE DUCHESS OF SUSSEX, Princess Ada Mazi Omu of Arochukwu, Princess Meghan Markle (43% Nigerian), and her impure children (<43% Nigerian)— **Habakkuk,** not feudal agriculture, lured the Italian Jewish ancestors of Benjamin Disraeli (1804–1881) to Great Britain. Prior to SLAVERY, there weren't very, very, very, many proper houses in BEDFORD.

"The supreme vice is shallowness." Wilde (1854–1900).

King's School and Oxbridge-educated, Lord Justice Charles Anthony Haddon-Cave, KC, a RACIST son of a very, very, very, rich Tasmanian Colonialist Economic Cannibal (**Mark 10:25**), an impostor and an expert of deception (perception is grander than reality), and a hereditary white supremacist descendant of DRUG LORDS (opium merchants of the Qing Dynasty), and a homie of Eton and Oxbridge-educated very, very, very, very, rich men's son, Archbishop Justin Welby (**Mark 10:25),** reasoning and vision do not have finite boundaries. The mind that I did not choose is finer than your unashamedly MEDIOCRE Fish and Chips Justice System, and I do not believe in any part of SHIT, as no part of SHIT is good, not even one— **Psalm 53**, and I have the POWER to use cogent facts and irrefutable evidence to irreparably destroy you and every part of SHIT – **Habakkuk 1:4:** OYINBO OLE/ODE.

Based on several decades of very, very, very, proximate observations and direct experiences, homogeneity in the administration of English Law is an impregnable secure mask of MERCILESS RACIST EVIL, an intelligently designed weapon of RACE WAR—**Habakkuk 1:4.**

RACIAL BIAS AND THE BENCH.

https://www.intermediaries-for-justice.org › files

In fact, there are currently no Black judges in the High. Court, Court of Appeal or Supreme Court. Not one. As Judge Peter Herbert stated: "The judiciary is …

"The 99% of the meetings I go to, I am the only non-white person in the room. But why are we so surprised when most of the senior positions in Scotland are filled exclusively by people who are White. Take my Portfolio alone, the Lord President, White. The Lord Justice Clerk, White. Every High Court Judge, White. The Lord Advocate, White. The Solicitor General, White. The Chief Constable, White. Every Deputy Chief Constable, White. Every Assistant Chief Constable, White. The head of the Law Society, White. The head of the faculty of advocates, White. Every Prison Governor, White. Not just Justice, the Chief Medical Officer, White. The Chief Nursing Officer, White. The Chief Veterinary Officer, White. he Chief Social Work Adviser, White. Almost every trade union in this country is headed by people who are White. In the Scottish Government, every director general is White, and every chair of every public body is White." A former Scottish First Minister.

One of the reasons why the GDP of the USA is about 10X bigger than that of the UK (>$30 trillion:>$3 trillion < $4 trillion) is that progressive colour-blind merit is not THE SUPREME VIRTUE in Great Britain.

Based on several decades of very, very, very, very, proximate observations and direct experiences, the pattern of merciless racist evil is the same everywhere in their Godforsaken racist hell hole. They don't want their own mentally gentler white children (OECD) and the pure white IMBECILES they shepherd (predominantly but not exclusively pure white) to know the TRUTH, which is that apart from our INFERIOR SKIN COLOUR that we neither made nor chose, and our inferior accent of speaking a foreign language, our own people (AFRICANS) are also properly created by Almighty God, and to conceal this TRUTH, and stifle individual unbounded development and unrestricted overall growth, the SAVE FACE—by CRIMINALLY stealing yields of our people's (AFRICANS) Christ-granted talents, and their unbounded, unaccountable, and overwhelming LEVERAGE is the certainty that all JUDGES would be PURE WHITE, and their hope is that they would be hereditary white supremacist bastards too—**Habakkuk 1:4.**

OYINBO OLE/ODE: BEDFORD, ENGLAND: GDC, Freemason, Brother Richard William Hill fabricated reports and unrelentingly lied under oath and on record—**Habakkuk 1:4.** The poor pure white ancestors of his pure white father and mother were incompetent RACIST LIARS too, like the pure white ancestors of King's School and Oxbridge-educated Lord Justice Charles Anthony Haddon-Cave, KC, a RACIST son of a very, very, very, RICH Tasmanian Colonialist Economic Cannibal (**Mark 10:25**), Sir Charles Phillip Haddon-Cave (1925–1999), an impostor and an expert of deception (perception is grander than reality), and a closeted hereditary white supremacist descendant of DRUG LORDS (Opium Merchants of the Qing Dynasty), and a homie of Eton and Oxbridge-educated rich men's son (**Mark 10:25**), Archbishop Justin Welby, they were THIEVES and owners of stolen children of defenceless poor people, including the pure black African ancestors of our IMPURE DUCHESS OF SUSSEX, Princess Ada Mazi Omu of Arochukwu, Princess Meghan Markle (43% Nigerian), and her impure children (<43% Nigerian)—**Habakkuk**.

A very, very, very, dishonest typical pure white Englishman. A closeted hereditary RACIST Freemason— Habakkuk. His type killed the NIGERIAN, only 56, and the INDIAN, only 42, albeit hands-off, with the mens rea hidden in the belly of the actus reus.

Google: Dr Richard Bamgboye, GP.

Google: Dr Anand Kamath, Dentist.

Leviticus 19:33–34: XENOPHOBIC HEREDITARY RACIST BASTARDS KILL FOREIGNERS, ONLY FOREIGNERS: INTELLIGENTLY DESIGNED QUASI-ETHNIC CLEANSING.

Based on several decades of very, very, very, proximate observations and direct experiences, they hate us, and we know, and they hate our children more, but they don't know.

Our own Mediocre, Wonky, Pure White Hereditary Racist, unashamedly functionally semi-illiterate, poly-educated poor man's son, a mere former debt-collector Solicitor in Norfolk/Norwich (5th Rate Partner), and the Senior Vice President of the Association of Her Majesty's District Judges, Bedford's District Judge Paul Robert Ayers, 3, St Paul's Square, MK 40 1SQ: It is me the hereditary RACIST pure white bastard wants, but it my daughter he got. The opportunist RACIST BASTARD should stay here, it is safer. There, we shall take revenge, and we shall destroy their children—a tooth for a tooth—**Exodus 21: 23–27.**

OYINBO OLE/ODE: TURF WAR: Descendants of ALIENS, with arbitrarily acquired camouflage English names—oppress NIGERIAN descendants of the ROBBED with yields of the ROBBERY—**Exodus 20:15.** Before Slavery, what? Then, they carried and sold millions of stolen children of defenceless poor people, now THIEVES steal our own NATURAL RESOURCES from our own AFRICA. No brain. Poor natural resources. Several continuous centuries of stealing and slavery preceded their HUGE STOLEN INHERITANCE—**Habakkuk.**

OYINBO OLE/ODE: Then, there was only subsistence feudal agriculture.

OYINBO OLE/ODE: "Agriculture not only gives riches to a nation, but the only one she can call her own." Dr Samuel Johnson (1709–1784).

******

NEGRO'S PERSPECTIVE:

If the NHS (Charlotte Dowling Goodson) had been requesting the 'HISTORY' (NHS reports), it meant that NHS did not have them, and there was no practitioners' file, and they were not in any file that was available to the NHS. Incompetently created reports that NHS (Charlotte Dowling Goodson) was waiting for—needed time for it to be created; that was what happened while they were requesting them—they were in synthesis.

Google: Mrs Charlotte Dowling (Goodson): Racist Lies and Letters of the Archetypal NHS Manager (2006).

They foresaw that a crooked and/or scatter-head hereditary RACIST pure white bastard who studied very, very, very, soft BUSINESS STUDIES at Poly (not Russell Group Inferior Alternative Education—Proverbs 17:16, would be a NHS Manager, so they used GUNS to loot and pillage Africa.

Mrs Charlotte Dowling (Goodson): Racist Lies and Letters ...

https://www.amazon.com › Mrs-Charlotte-Dowling-Go...

Mrs Charlotte Dowling (Goodson): Racist Lies and Letters of the Archetypal NHS Manager (2006): A Hired Racist Liar.: Great Britain: The Serengeti of.

US$12.65

INCOMPETENT RACIST LIES. The Histories of the Hereditary Racist Pure White Bastards are Brainless and Baseless Stories.

"To survive, you must tell stories." Umberto Eco (1932–2016).

Our Lord Justice of pure white IMBECILES (predominantly but not exclusively pure white) of our Empire of STOLEN INHERITANCE, an impostor and an expert of deception (perception is grander than reality), King's School and Oxbridge-educated Lord Justice Charles Anthony Haddon-Cave, KC, a RACIST son of a very, very, very, RICH Tasmanian Colonialist Economic Cannibal (**Mark 10:25**), Sir Charles Phillip Haddon-Cave (1925–1999), and closeted hereditary white supremacist descendant of DRUG LORDS (Opium Merchants of the Qing Dynasty), and a homie of Eton and Oxbridge-educated rich men's son (**Mark 10:25**), Archbishop Justin Welby, having FAILED in practice, his father did too, the pure white privileged dullards parked their liabilities at the public till: PRIVILEGED DULLARDS' QUASI-DOLE.

Lord Leon Brittan (1939-2015): "A German Jew." Lord Denning (1899-1999).

SEVEN: ENDURING RESIDUES OF THE ROLE OF DALIT-BUFFERS IN EXPLOITATIVE ECONOMICALLY CANNIBALISTIC COLONISATION OF AFRICA, AND THE ONGOING NEOCOLONIALISM.

"Jesus is the bedrock of my faith." HM (1926–2022): Antichrist hereditary RACIST pure white bastards (predominantly but not exclusively pure white) find a very, very, very, dull Coconut Dalit, preferably a physically ill-favoured and mentally wonky cow worshipper (**John 14:6),** and they adorned him very, very, very, high titles, and he becomes Antichrist Freemasons' Private Soldier (MEDIOCRE MAFIA)—**Habakkuk 1:4.**

"I think I will ask our legal adviser for any advice he may have. My view is that there are six or seven of us here who had the admission down, but we cannot find it in the transcript and there is wordings that imply that there was, but it is not in black and white…..." Shiv Pabary, Member of the Most Excellent Order of our Empire (MBE), the Archetypal GDC Committee Chairperson, and Justice of Peace (JP).

BRAINLESS RACIST NONSENSE.

THE YIELD OF THE VERY, VERY, VERY, ELEMENTARY MIND OF OUR BRAINLESS, SCATTER-HEAD, HEDITARY RACIST, AND CROOKED IMPOSTOR AND EXPERT OF DECEPTION, LOWLIFE COCONUT DALIT, ALBEIT A MEMBER OF THE MOST EXCELLENT ORDER OF OUR EMPIRE OF STOLEN INHERITANCE—**HABAKKUK**.

INCESTUOUSLY CONCEIVED ANTICHRIST COCONUT DALITS HAVE IMPOSED IRREPARABLE

MEDIOCRITY AND CONFUSION OF GREAT BRITAIN.

GOOGLE: MEDIOCRE GDC.

Based on cogent, irrefutable, and available evidence, Shiv Pabary, Member of the Most Excellent Order of our Empire (MBE), the Archetypal GDC Committee Chairperson, and Justice of Peace (JP), unrelentingly lied under oath and on record—**Habakkuk 1:4.** We are all who we are, the inheritors of our inheritances, genes of individual ancestors. His mother and father must have been incompetent RACIST LIARS too.

They lie that they don't lie—**Psalm 144. Psalm 116:11:** "Lies are told all the time." Sir Mr Justice Robert Michael Havers (1923–1992), QC, Oxbridge-educated very, very, very, very, rich man's son (**Mark 10:25**).

Then, our own Premier, the Scholar from FIFE, could not spell; in our own Country of the BLIND, the partially sighted was our shepherd. DYSLEXIA is part Atypical Dementia and Alzheimer's disease.

Then, our own PREMIER, a Coconut Dalit, albeit a loaded one, our torchbearer, worshipped cows with MILK, not bulls with no milk: **John 14:6**.

"Truth, Sir, is the cow that would yield such people no milk, so they are gone to milk the bull." Dr Samuel Johnson (1709–1784).

A Gong is not a Nobel Prize, so a brainless impostor and expert of deception, an ignorant, crooked, mediocre, and RACIST Pakistani-looking Coconut Dalit—bagged it.

[Prince Charles wants to shake up honours system when he …](https://www.dailymail.co.uk)

https://www.dailymail.co.uk › news › article-2933738

2 Feb 2015—The heir to the throne believes gongs are handed out 'to the wrong people for the wrong reasons'. He is said to want to scrap honours such as ...

"I think I will ask our legal adviser for any advice he may have. My view is that there are six or seven of us here who had the admission down." Shiv Pabary

BRAINLESS RACIST NONSENSE.

KULI ODE: The PAKISTANI looking Coconut Dalit lied. If all Bradford's Imams, and all Newcastle's Gurus could disprove the TRUTH that Shiv Pabary (MBE) unrelentingly lied under oath and on record they will confirm the belief of lots and lots of people that INCESTUOUS CONCEPTION is unrelated to atypical dementia.

"Starmer speech on Britain becoming 'Island of strangers' is fundamentally racist." Diane Abbott

Everyone came, including the Saxe-Coburg, and Gotha family, and they arbitrarily acquired a camouflage English name in 1917.

TURF WAR: Keir Starmer and his type, GENETIC ALIENS, oppress African descendants of the robbed with yields of the ROBBERY—**Habakkuk.** Before Slavery, what? Equitable, fair, and just REPARATION pends, and several centuries of unpaid interest accrue.

Based on cogent, irrefutable, and available evidence, their unashamedly MEDIOCRE Fish and Chips Justice System is irreparably FU*KED, it has foreseeably succumbed to INCEST, weakening of the common genetic pool, and associated physical and mental wonkiness, and hereditary white supremacist FREEMASON JUDGES, and others. who make loads of money from unashamed mediocrity and confusion PROP SHIT UP: Conflict of interest.

"A government that robs Peter to pay Paul can always depend on the support of Paul." George Bernard Shaw (1856–1950).

Matthew 12:27: Reporting a pure white hereditary racist pure white Freemason Criminal to a pure white hereditary RACIST Freemason Judge is akin to reporting a Green-eyed demon to a Blue-eyed devil.

THE BOTTOM IS THE NEW TOP: If the bottom descends to the basement, and the top simultaneously descends to the bottom, there will be harmonious change without relative change because the distance between the basement (the former bottom) and the bottom (the former top) will remain the same. The former top is oblivious to the notion of relativity, so it has refused to accept that it is the NEW BOTTOM. Contrariwise, If the bottom descends to the basement, and the top ascends higher up, there will be disharmonious FRACTURE because the distance between the basement (the former bottom) and the higher top (the former top) will increase. Disharmonious fracture is more progressive than collective decline.

GDC: Helen Falcon (MBE), Community Dentist, Dishonest ...

https://www.amazon.co.uk › GDC-Community-Dishone...

" Dr Shiv Pabary, Member of the British Empire (MBE) and Justice of ... mediocre, institutionally racist, vindictive, and weaponised system that is ...

£14.73

The fact that an incestuously conceived, brainless impostor and expert of deception, ignorant, crooked, mediocre, and RACIST Pakistani-looking Coconut Dalit was the best student in your school is not proof that he was a GENIUS, but it is proof that you are CRAP. as better than crap is crap.

One of the reasons why the GDP of the USA is about 10X bigger than the GDP of the UK (>$30 trillion: >3<$4 trillion) is that brainless impostors and experts of deception, ignorant, crooked, mediocre, and RACIST Pakistani-looking Coconut Dalits are paid the salaries of GDC Committee Chairpersons.

Brainless impostors and experts of deception, ignorant, crooked, mediocre, and RACIST Pakistani-looking Coconut Dalits are dragging Britain down: Substance is subservient to superfluous.

"………we cannot find it in the transcript and there is wordings that imply that there was…" Shiv Pabary, Uncle Tom, a Scatter-head Coconut Dalit, Justice of Peace, Member of the Most Excellent Order of our Empire of Stolen Inheritance – **Habakkuk**, and the archetypal GDC Committee Chairperson.

KULI ODE: AN IMBECILE DALIT: AN ADULT DALIT WITH THE BASIC SKILLS OF A CHILD: SCORES OF MILLIONS OF HIS COUSINS GO TO THE BUSH TO SHIT IN PUNJAB. PERCEPTION IS GRANDER THAN REALITY.

If all the Gurus in Gujarat, and all the Imams in Newcastle, and all the Rabbis in Bradford, and all the Freemasons in Birmingham could disprove the TRUTH, which is that our physically ill-favoured, mentally wonky (probably incestuously conceived), and RACIST Pakistani-looking Coconut Dalit lied under oath and/or on record— **Habakkuk 1:4,** Shiv Pabary, MBE, lied under oath when he stated: "…we cannot find it in the transcript and there is wordings that imply that there was…", they will confirm the belief of billions of people in our world, which is that Antichrist Islam, Antichrist Judaism, Antichrist Freemasonry Quasi-Religion (Mediocre Racist Mafia), including religions and faiths associated with the 15 Holy

Books in the House of Commons, and all other motley assemblies of exotic religions and faiths under the common umbrella of the Governor of the Church of England, and the Defender of the Faith—**John 14:6,** are not intellectually flawed SATANIC MUMBO JUMBO.

John 14:6: "Jesus is the bedrock of my faith." HM (1926–2022): Defenders of FAITHS are dissenters of the faith.

Rashpal Singh Mondair: A Racist Dalit is the Archetypal GDC ...

https://www.amazon.com › zh_TW

·Translate this page

Rashpal Singh Mondair: A Racist Dalit is the Archetypal GDC Committee Chairperson. Maharajah Shiv Pabary (MBE), a Nigg*r's Encounters.: Matthew 12:27:

One of the reasons why the GDP of the USA is about 10X the GDP of the UK (>$30 trillion:>3<$4 trillion) is that brainless impostors and experts of deception, ignorant, crooked, mediocre, and RACIST Pakistani-looking Coconut Dalits like Rashpal Singh Mondair was paid the salary of the GDC Committee Chairperson.

Google: Mediocre GDC. Facts are sacred and cannot be overstated.

Google: Rashpal Singh Mondair: A Racist Dalit is the Archetypal GDC Committee Chairperson. Maharajah.

OUR OWN NIGERIA, SHELL'S DOCILE CASH COW SINCE1956 (OLOIBIRI). GDC WAS ESTABLISHED IN 1956.

Very, very, very, very, very, bellyful Rashpal Singh Mondair, Dentist: A brainless, crooked, and hereditary RACIST Pakistani looking Coconut Dalit, whose father and mother have never seen CRUDE OIL was granted the platform to display hereditary prejudice. They are the BEST in everything, but only where superfluous is subservient to substance.

COLONIAL AFRICA: Dalits, thoroughly wretched untouchables became Maharajahs, and they were very, very, very, very, very, happy with every position underneath a pure white woman if armed pure white men placed them above all NEGROES in the pecking order.

"One witness at the Royal Commission in 1897 said that the ambition of Indians in Trinidad was to buy a cow, then a shop, and say: 'We are no Nigg*rs to work in cane fields.'" Patrick French's Book, 'The World Is What It Is: The Authorised Biography of V.S Naipaul.

"Shithole Africa." President Trump

King's School and Oxbridge-educated Lord Justice Charles Anthony Haddon-Cave, KC, a RACIST son of a very, very, very, RICH Tasmanian Colonialist Economic Cannibal (**Mark 10:25**), Sir Charles Phillip Haddon-Cave (1925–1999), and a properly schooled impostor and an expert of deception (perception is grander than reality), and a closeted hereditary white supremacist descendant of DRUG LORDS (Opium Merchants of the Qing Dynasty), and a homie of Eton and Oxbridge-educated rich men's son (**Mark 10:25**), Archbishop Justin Welby, the mind that the NIGERIAN, from shithole AFRICA, did not choose is FINER than your unashamedly MEDIOCRE Fish and Chips JUSTICE SYSTEM, and he does not believe in any part of SHIT, as no part of SHIT is good, not even one—**Psalm 53**, and he has the POWER to use cogent facts and irrefutable evidence to irreparably destroy you and every part of SHIT—**Habakkuk 1:4**. Facts are sacred and cannot be overstated.

OXFORD, ENGLAND: GDC, British Soldier, Stephanie Twidale (TD), A GONG HUNTER, unrelentingly lied under oath and on record—**Habakkuk 1:4.** The poor pure white ancestors of her pure white father and mother were incompetent RACIST LIARS too, like the pure white ancestors of King's School and Oxbridge-educated Lord Justice Charles Anthony Haddon-Cave, KC, a RACIST son of a very, very, very, RICH Tasmanian Colonialist Economic Cannibal (**Mark 10:25),** Sir Charles Phillip Haddon-Cave (1925–1999), and a properly schooled impostor and an expert of deception (perception is grander than reality), and a closeted hereditary white supremacist descendant of DRUG LORDS (Opium Merchants of the Qing Dynasty), and a homie of Eton and Oxbridge-educated rich men's son (**Mark 10:25**), Archbishop Justin Welby, they were THIEVES and owners of stolen children of defenceless poor people, including the pure black African ancestors of our IMPURE DUCHESS OF SUSSEX, Princess Ada Mazi Omu of Arochukwu, Princess Meghan Markle (43% Nigerian), and her impure children (<43% Nigerian)—Habakkuk.

A very, very, very, dishonest typical pure white Englishwoman. A crooked closeted hereditary RACIST British Soldier—**Habakkuk**. Her type killed the NIGERIAN, only 56, and the INDIAN, only 42, albeit hands-off, with the mens rea hidden in the belly of the actus reus.

Google: Dr Richard Bamgboye, GP. Google: Dr Anand Kamath, Dentist.

The YANKS are NATO, and absolutely everything else is an auxiliary bluff.

1944: about 1.5 million of American Soldiers were in Great Britain, and about 200,000 of them were NEGROES. Tens of thousands of descendants of SLAVES died, in Europe, in the pursuant of the continuing propagation of descendants of SLAVE OWNERS.

Luke 11:52: They lied to their own mentally gentler white children (OECD) and the pure white imbeciles they shepherd (predominantly but not exclusively pure white) that they are ultra-righteous GENIUSES, very, very, very, highly civilised, and SUPER-ENLIGHTENED, and they do everything LEGALLY: Rules-based procedures, precedent, statute etcetera, including RACIAL HATRED and FRAUD—**Habakkuk 1:4.** Integrity, friendship, respect, and charity: All for one, and one for all. Defenders of FAITHS are dissenters of the FAITH, and the hereditary white supremacist bastards are closeted enemies of the SOVEREIGN, the Defender of the Faith—**John 14:6.**

Reasoning and vision do not have finite boundaries. The fellow is who He says He is—**John 14:6.** The supernatural exists and it is consistently accessible to those who stand where it can come—**John 14:26.** King's School and Oxbridge-educated Lord Justice Charles Anthony Haddon-Cave, KC, a RACIST son of a very, very, very, RICH Tasmanian Colonialist Economic Cannibal (**Mark 10:25**), Sir Charles Phillip Haddon-Cave (1925–1999), and a properly schooled impostor and an expert of deception (perception is grander than reality), and a closeted hereditary white supremacist descendant of DRUG LORDS (Opium Merchants of the Qing Dynasty), and a homie of Eton and Oxbridge-educated rich men's son (**Mark 10:25**), Archbishop Justin Welby, I have the POWER to use cogent facts and irrefutable evidence to irreparably DESTROY you and your unashamedly MEDIOCRE Fish and Chips Justice system, and all the MONEY in the world will not repair SHIT, and it will be in the PUBLIC INTEREST to do so, as part of His face will be uncovered—**John 14:6.**

OYINBO OLE: PURE WHITE EUROPEAN CHRISTIAN, KING LEOPOLD'S GHOST: RACIAL HATRED, GREED, TERROR, RACIST MURDER, AND ECONOMIC CANNIBALISM IN AFRICA—BY EVIL PURE WHITE EUROPEAN CHRISTIAN BASTARDS - **HABAKKUK.**

"How Europe underdeveloped Africa." Dr Walter Rodney (1942–1980).

"The white man is the devil." Elijah Mohammed (1897–1975).

OYINBO OLE/ODE: Pure White European Christians invented Antichrist hereditary white supremacist Satanic Network in the early 18th century, about 1717, at a height of European Christians' EVIL, but very, very, very, PROFITABLE SADISTIC COMMERCE in millions of STOLEN CHILDREN of defenceless poor people, including the pure Black African ancestors of the IMPURE (<43% Nigerian) great grandchildren of the Duke of Edinburgh of Blessed Memory, Prince Phillip (1921-2021)

Philippians 1:21: Phillip was a 33rd Degree Freemason (Scottish Rite).

LAWYERS' SCAM: Keir Starmer, Diane Abbott, Mrs Thatcher, Kemi Badenoch, Kamala Harris, Davis Lammy, Barack Obama Etcetera: When Lawyers FAILED in practice, loads did, if they were MASONS or if not. they always parked their liabilities at the PUBLIC TILL, and other people paid them loads of other people's money—in exchange for unashamed mediocrity and confusion, and in pursuant of continuing propagation of PURE WHITE IMBECILES (predominantly but not exclusively pure white adults with the basic skills of a child): QUASI-COMMUNISM.

"I emphasis the point." Our own Mediocre, Wonky, Pure White Hereditary Racist, unashamedly functionally semi-illiterate, poly-educated poor man's son, a mere former debt-collector Solicitor in Norfolk/Norwich (5th Rate Partner), and the Senior Vice President of the Association of Her Majesty's District Judges, Bedford's District Judge Paul Robert Ayers, 3, St Paul's Square, MK 40 1SQ.

John 8:7, Matthew 7:1–6: A brainless hereditary RACIST pure white bastard sat on a very, very, very, expensive highchair that his own pure white mother and father could not afford, and which the pure white imbeciles who sat before him (predominantly but not exclusively pure white) could not, and did not, buy—in their GRAND COURT that was preceded by SLAVERY, future flats and absolutely inevitable distant future's NUCLEAR ASH, and the opportunist RACIST pure white bastard Judged SINNERS.

John 5:22: Only He who has no sin has the MORAL RIGHT to Judge SINNERS> God Almighty Judges no one, but only the sinless creator has the MORAL RIGHT to appoint sinless Judges—to Judge Sinners. Descendants of THIEVES do not have the MORAL RIGHT to Judge AFRICANS, especially when equitable, fair, and just REPARATION pends, and several continuous centuries of unpaid interest accrue.

OYINBO OLE/ODE: "All have taken what had other owners and all have had recourse to arms rather than quit the prey onto which they were fastened." Dr Samuel Johnson (1709–1784).

OYINBO OLE/ODE: "It was in 1066 that William the Conqueror occupied Britain, stole our land and granted it to his Norman friends thus the feudal system, which we have not yet fully escaped." Tony Benn (1925–2014).

Mark 10:25: Elon Musk: Hereditary Intra-Racial Sex Machine.

EIGHT: Psalm 53: No one is good, not even one. William the Conqueror stole from others what others stole from others.

OYINBO OLE/ODE: Based on cogent, irrefutable, and available evidence, SLAVERY rebuilt everything it succeeded and paid for everything it preceded, including ANEURIN BEVAN'S NHS (1948), and DAME MARGARET SEWARD'S GDC (1956).

"The fact is, that civilisation requires slaves. The Greeks were quite right there. Unless there are slaves to do the ugly, horrible, uninteresting work, culture and contemplation become almost impossible. Human slavery is wrong, insecure, and demoralising......" Wilde (1854–1900).

Exodus 21:23–27: If our own Mediocre, Wonky, Pure White Hereditary Racist, unashamedly functionally semi-illiterate, poly-educated poor man's son, a mere former debt-collector Solicitor in Norfolk/Norwich (5th Rate Partner), and the Senior Vice President of the Association of Her Majesty's District Judges, Bedford's District Judge Paul Robert Ayers, 3, St Paul's Square, MK 40 1SQ, were to do a TOURIST WALK ABOUT in our own tribe in African bush, the probability that the evil opportunist RACIST pure white bastard would be castrated, without anaesthesia, and lynched like Gadhafi—for the sins of his ancestors—is greater than minus 100% (>-100%). The hereditary RACIST pure white bastard, albeit England's Class Senior District Judge, should fu*king stay here, it is safer. There, he would be FORCED to pay for the sins of Merciless Racist Pure White Bastard Ancestors, but only LEGALLY, under our own native and customary laws.

OYINBO OLE/ODE: Coster family of SWANSEA, Richard Pennant (the First Baron Penrhyn), W. Nathaniel Wells

Etcetera were EVIL WELSH SLAVE MERCHANTS. Part of the RESULTANT effects of several continuous centuries of STEALING and SLAVERY was that a crooked pure white Welsh bastard was our Senior Welsh Postgraduate Tutor, Oxford.

Letters of a Racist Crooked Imbecile Welsh Dentist, Geraint
https://www.amazon.co.uk › Letters-Crooked-Imbecile-...
Geraint. R. Evans – BDS (Bham), MSc GDP, Cert Clin Ed, Cert Implant: Letters and Lies of a Crooked Racist Welsh Imbecile. Google: Mediocre GDC.
£10.44.

Just as it was in Professor Stephen Hawking's School, then, at the University of Lagos, the brightest students did mathematics, physics, and chemistry, and did not attend lectures at the Faculty of Law.

"In my school, the brightest boys did math and physics, the less bright did physics and chemistry, and the least bright did biology. I wanted to do math and physics, but my father made me do chemistry because he thought there would be no jobs for mathematicians." Dr Stephen Hawking (1942–2018).

Their grossly overrated, overhyped, overpopulated, and MEDIOCRE TRADE that is dying slowly and imperceptibly, and is overseen by the Antichrist Racist Freemasons (Mediocre Mafia, New Pharisees—**Luke 11:52**, New Good Samaritans (**Luke 10:25–37**), New Good Shepherd (**John 10:11–18**), and New Truly Good God (**Mark 10:18**). Defenders of Faiths are Dissenter of the Faith, and closeted fundamental enemies of the Sovereign, the Defender of the FAITH – **John 14:6.**

Our own Mediocre, Wonky, Pure White Hereditary Racist, unashamedly functionally semi-illiterate, poly-educated poor man's son, a mere former debt-collector Solicitor in

Norfolk/Norwich (5th Rate Partner), and the Senior Vice President of the Association of Her Majesty's District Judges, Bedford's District Judge Paul Robert Ayers, 3, St Paul's Square, MK 40 1SQ, an ignorant descendant of MERCILESS RACIST MURDERERS, liars, THIEVES and owners of stolen children of defenceless poor people, including the pure Black African ancestors of the IMPURE (<43% Nigerian) niece and nephew of the Prince of Wales.— **Habakkuk; John 8:44; John 10:10.**

Properly rehearsed ultra-righteousness and deceptively schooled civilised decorum were preceded by several continuous centuries of MERCILESS RACIST EVIL: The greediest economic cannibalism and the evilest RACIST TERRORISM the world will ever know - **Habakkuk.**

Habakkuk 2:5: Based on several decades of very, very, very, proximate observations and direct experiences, they are greedier than the grave, and like death, the evil RACIST BASTARDS can never be satisfied.

"England is like a prostitute who, having sold her body all her life, decides to close her business, and then tells everybody that she wants to protect her flesh as if it were jade." He Manzi (1919–2009).

OYINBO OLE/ODE: "Many Scots masters were considered among the most brutal, with life expectancy on their plantations averaging a mere four years. We worked them to death then simply imported more to keep the sugar and thus the money flowing. Unlike centuries of grief and murder, an apology cost nothing. So, what does Scotland have to say?" Herald Scotland: Ian Bell, Columnist, Sunday 28 April 2013

OYINBO OLE/ODE: Evil RACIST pure white bastards are no longer here, but their evil mutant genes of sadism and savagery flow through the veins of their more evil direct descendants who remain here—**Habakkuk.**

"The legal system lies at the heart of any society, protecting rights, imposing duties, and establishing a framework for the conduct of almost every social, political, and economic activity. Some argue that the law is in its death throes while others postulate a contrary prognosis that discerns numerous signs of law's enduring strength. Which is it?" Professor Raymond Wacks, Emeritus Professor of Law, Hong Kong

"……..we cannot find it in the transcript and there is wordings that imply that there was, but it is not in black and white." Shiv Pabary, Crooked, Scatter-head, closeted racist bastard, MBE, JP, and the Archetypal GDC Committee Chairperson.

BRAINLESS RACIST NONSENSE:

A properly schooled impostor and an expert of deception was granted the platform to display hereditary prejudice.

The incompetently DISHONEST hereditary bastard was a 'Professor' at Newcastle University. Their scatter-head Dalit, an impostor and an expert of deception, sells unashamed mediocrity and confusion to the undiscerning.

Sheep unnaturally shepherd sheep. Shepherds know that sheep are MORONS, but sheep do not know that shepherds are MORONS too.

"Mediocrity weighing mediocrity in the balance, and incompetence applauding its brother………" Wilde (1854–1900)

The most important part of the matter is MONEY, and it is not the yield of his very, very, very, HIGH IQ, and unlike PUTIN'S RUSSIA, there are no oil wells oil wells or gas fields in GUJARAT, PUNJAB, NEWCASTLE, and where the father and mother of Shiv Pabary, Member of the Most Excellent Order of our Empire Stolen Inheritance— **Habakkuk,** were born.

If their scatter-head, crooked, and closeted RACIST Dalit bastard could not find it in the Official Legal Transcript, it was because it was in the UNOFFICIAL ILLEGAL TRANSCRIPT. and if there were wordings that implied there were, but not in BLACK and WHITE, they must have been written RED, GOLD, BLACK, AND GREEN - Steel Pulse.

KULI ODE: A MORON DALIT, ALBEIT A MEMBER OF THE MOST EXCELLENT ORDER OF OUR EMPIRE OF STOLEN INHERITANCE – **HABAKKUK.** BEFORE SLAVERY, WHAT?

One of the reasons why the GDC of the USA is about 10X bigger than that of the UK (>$30 trillion: >$3 trillion < $4 trillion) is that SHIV PABARY, MBE, lowlife, crooked, and closeted RACIST COCONUT DALIT was paid the salary of the Archetypal GDC Committee Chairperson.

Google: Evlynne Gilvarry, Institutionally Racist GDC.

Evlynne Gilvarry: Institutionally Racist GDC, Incompetent …

https://www.amazon.co.uk › Evlynne-Gilvarry-Instituti…

Buy Evlynne Gilvarry: Institutionally Racist GDC, Incompetent Racist Lies, and Regulating African Dentists.: Rashpal Singh Mondair: Archetypal GDC Committee …

£16.13 · In stock · 30-day returns,

GONG HUNTERS: The GONG isn't a NOBEL PRIZE, so scatter-head Dalits can bag it.

The brainless, crooked, and RACIST Dalit impersonated a Maharajah.

"Rally round the flag. Rally round the Red, Gold, Black and Green. Marcus say, Sir Marcus say Red for the blood that flowed like the river. Marcus say, Sir Marcus say Green for the land Africa. Marcus say Yellow for the Gold that they stole. Marcus say Black for the people it was looted from. They took us away captivity, captivity. Required from us a song. Right now, man say repatriate, repatriate. I and I patience have now long time gone ......" Steel Pulse.

KULI OLE/ODE: A DISHONEST CLOSETED RACIST MEMBER OF THE MOST EXCELLENT ORDER OF OUR OWN EMPIRE OF STOLEN INHERITANCE—HABAKKUK.

Based on very proximate observations and direct experiences, Shiv Pabary, MBE, looked physically ill-favoured and mentally wonky, and according to the NEWS, his brother is wonky too, certainly mentally: Their mother and father could be related (siblings or cousins). Charles Darwin (1809–1882) married his first cousin, and expectedly, their children, not all, were physically and/or mentally wonky, and some of them were so wonky, they died in UTERO.

Albert Einstein (1879–1955) married his first cousin, and their children were so wonky, they all died IN UTERO.

OUR OWN NIGERIA, SHELL'S DOCILE CASH COW SINCE 1956 (OLOIBIRI). GDC WAS ESTABLISHED IN 1956.

Our own NIGERIAN BABIES with huge oil wells and gas fields near their huts eat only 1.5/day in our own NIGERIA, very, very, very, bellyful incestuously conceived bastards, including scatter-head, crooked, and closeted RACIST Shiv Pabary, Member of the Most Excellent Order of our Empire of STOLEN INHERITANCE—thrive in 'ASIANS' COUNTRY', the North of England, the Serengeti of incestuously conceived Pakistanis.

ACCURATE SEERS: They foresaw that scatter-head, crooked, and closeted RACIST Shiv Pabary, Member of the Most Excellent Order of our Empire of STOLEN INHERITANCE, would be the Archetypal GDC Committee Chairperson, so they embarked on armed robbery and dispossession in AFRICA: Wherever they mercilessly slaughtered AFRICANS, they dispossessed them, and whenever they robbed our own direct ancestors, they took possession, and they used HUGE YIELDS of several continuous centuries of MERCILESS RACIST EVIL, the greediest economic cannibalism and the EVILEST RACIST TERRORISM the world will ever know to create a very, very, very, LAVISH SOCIALIST ELDORADO for imbeciles, including incestuously conceived IMBECILES, and they decommissioned natural selection, and they reversed progressive evolution, and they made it possible for millions of IMBECILES to breed more millions of IMBECILES, including physically and/or mentally wonky incestuous conceived mentally subhuman bastards.

SIR KEIR STARMER: As progressive evolution and its driver, Natural Selection, were INVENTED by God, why is using NUCLEAR BOMBS to preserve the continuing propagation of incestuously conceived physically and/or mentally wonky Britons, not ANTICHRIST? What does Great Britain need those who natural selection would have deselected had it not been decommissioned—for?

"Natural selection will not remove ignorance from future generations." Dr Richard Dawkins.

"We have decommissioned natural selection……." Dr E.O. Wilson (1929–2021).

OUR OWN NIGERIA: SHELL'S DOCILE CASH COW SINCE 1956 (OLOIBIRI). GDC WAS ESTABLISHED IN 1956.

Our own NIGERIAN BABIES with huge oil wells and gas fields near their huts eat only 1.5/day in our own NIGERIA, two, only two, but two too many very, very, very, bellyful, physically ill-favoured and or mental wonky Pakistani-looking Dalits, Shiv Pabary, Member of the Most Excellent Order of our own Empire of STOLEN INHERITANCE—Habakkuk, and his biological brother—whose mother and father have never seen CRUDE OIL thrive in Great Britain. Which part of our own SHITHOLE Africa is great?

"Sometimes people don't want to hear the truth because they don't want their illusions destroyed." Friedrich Nietzsche (1844–1900).

******

"History will favour me, for I intend to write it." Sir Winston Churchill (1874–1965).

History should be an accurate record of the past. 'This decision was made against a history of noncompliance with legislation.' Charlotte Dowling Goodson (NHS) and Richard Hill (NHS), 30.07.2007

There was no 'HISTORY', as the reports that Sue Gregory (OBE), John Hooper (NHS) and Charlotte Dowling Goodson (NHS) requested or ordered were freshly fabricated reports (22.07.2004 and follow up of undisclosed date). They were abruptly withdrawn on 16.10.2008, more than four years after the alleged visits.

"To survive, you must tell stories." Umberto Eco (1932–2016).

On 30.07.2007, when Poly-educated Charlotte Dowling Goodson, England's Class NHS Manager, and the She-She Man Looking Man, Richard Hill, wrote down their incompetently fabricated NHS RACIST STORIES, at least three NHS fabrications were accessible to PURE WHITE

PEOPLE, and those who were in very, very, very, advanced stages in the metamorphosis of becoming PURE WHITE (PUPA):

1. The fabricated NHS report of July 22, 2004.

2. The fabricated NHS follow up report of undisclosed date.

3. The fabricated Email Address, of January 04, 2007, which its Poly-educated creator, expectedly never employed. On January 04, 2007, when Poly-educated Charlotte Dowling Goodson fabricated the Email Address, two other NHS Racist fabrications were accessible to hereditary RACIST pure white bastards, and those who were in very, very, very, advanced stages in the metamorphosis of becoming PURE WHITE (PUPA).

OYINBO OLE/ODE: "I have seen evil, and it has the face of Mark Fuhrman." Johnnie Cochran (1937–2005),

Like Poly-educated Charlotte Dowling (Goodson), not Russell Group Inferior Class Alternative Education— **Proverbs 17:16,** Mark Fuhrman (LAPD), half-educated school dropout GED, was PURE WHITE, but Archie is impure (<43% Nigerian)—**Habakkuk.**

The freshly fabricated, immoral and immortal, reckless and mendacious NHS reports of 22.07.2004 and follow up of undisclosed date have no useful historical content, before and after they were withdrawn.

They were all PURE WHITE: Homogeneity in the administration of English Law is an impregnable secure mask of MERCILESS RACIST EVIL, an intelligently designed weapon of RACE WAR.

Sue Gregory (OBE) was the cardinal of confusions.

'Study history, study history. In history lies all the secrets of statecraft.' Sir Winston Churchill (1874-1965).

Sir Winston Churchill did not refer to a recklessly fabricated account or record that was requested or ordered by sheep that needed shepherds, but impersonated shepherds.

Sue Gregory (OBE), Charlotte Dowling Goodson (NHS) and Richard Hill (NHS) were thoroughly confused. Brainless crooked racist pure white bastards GANGED UP to do merciless RACIST EVIL, but the pure white bastards were incompetent RACIST LIARS, and they were too dull to do RACIST EVIL seamlessly, as their incompetent art incompetently imitated life. Their type killed the Nigerian, only 56. and the Indian, only 42, albeit hands-off with the mens rea hidden in the belly of the actus reus.

Leviticus 19:33–34: They kill foreigners, only foreigners, albeit hands-off, with the mens rea hiffen in the belly of the actud reus.

Google: Dr Richard Bamgboye, GP.

Google: Dr Anand Kamath, Dentist.

Exodus 21:23–27: It is not the truth that they are the only ones who know how to kill people (Exodus 2013). They should stay here, it is safer. In Nigeria, we shall take revenge, and only under the LAW, God's Law: A tooth for a tooth, and a life for a life.

BEDFORD,ENGLAND: Our own Mediocre, Wonky, Pure White Hereditary Racist, unashamedly functionally semi-illiterate, poly-educated poor man's son, a mere former debt-collector Solicitor in Norfolk/Norwich (5th Rate Partner), and the Senior Vice President of the Association of Her Majesty's District Judges, Bedford's District Judge Paul Robert Ayers, 3, St Paul's Square, MK 40 1SQ, a brainless hereditary RACIST pure white bastard approved what his pure white mother spoke, a mere lowlife genetic alien with an arbitrarily acquired camouflage English name. The hereditary RACIST pure white bastard should stay here, it's safer. ONLY his superior SKIN COLOUR and Almighty God are truly good—**Mark 10:18**, and the opportunist RACIST pure white bastard, albeit England's Class SENIOR JUDGE neither made nor chose it, and the poly-educated pure white RUBBISH will be considerably diminished as a human being without it, and he knows it.

Exodus 21:23–27: In NIGERIA, the opportunist RACIST pure white bastard will be ROBUSTLY deterred from excessive stupidity.

"There is no sin except stupidity." Wilde (1854–1900).

BEDFORD, ENGLAND: Our own Mediocre, Wonky, Pure White Hereditary Racist, unashamedly functionally semi-illiterate, poly-educated poor man's son, a mere former debt-collector Solicitor in Norfolk/Norwich (5th Rate Partner), and the Senior Vice President of the Association of Her Majesty's District Judges, Bedford's District Judge Paul Robert Ayers, 3, St Paul's Square, MK 40 1SQ, unlike PUTIN'S RUSSIA, there are no oil wells or gas fields in FREEMASONS' KEMPSTON and where your own pure white father and mother were born. You have some of the characteristics THIEF. You weaponised your unashamedly MEDIOCRE Fish and Chips Justice System and cowardly indiscreetly use it as an instrument of RACE WAR.

"Those who have robbed have also lied." Dr Samuel Johnson (1709–1784).

Our own Mediocre, Wonky, Pure White Hereditary Racist, unashamedly functionally semi-illiterate, poly-educated poor man's son, a mere former debt-collector Solicitor in Norfolk/Norwich (5th Rate Partner), and the Senior Vice President of the Association of Her Majesty's District

Judges, Bedford's District Judge Paul Robert Ayers, 3, St Paul's Square, MK 40 1SQ, the most important part of the matter is MONEY, and it is not the yield of your very, very, very, HIGH IQ, and unlike PUTIN'S RUSSIA, there are no oil wells or gas fields in bland and colourless NORFOLK/NORWICH (Coastal Dole) and where your own pure white father and mother were born, and the very, very, very, highly luxuriant soil of Bishop's Stortford yields only FOOD. Bishop's Stortford Cecil Rhodes (1853–1902) was a RACIST pure white bastard, a murderer, an armed land grabber, and a professional thief – **Exodus 20:15.**

Standards are too low. Significant decline in educational standard is stifling almost every part with confusion. Black people will be 'eaten' first, but not last.

****

GDC CHAMBERS, 18.11.2008: ANDREW HURST (BARRISTER THAT WAS INSTRUCTED BY THE GDC): Although these are not within the Committee's bundle, is it right that you were asked by a colleague at the PCT to provide your previous practice inspection reports or visit reports so that Ms Twidale would have them in advance. Is that right?

RICHARD HILL (NHS): I don't think so, no. I think that's a wrong reading of it. I don't think that we did anything of the sort. I don't think she read any of those—in my knowledge, according to my knowledge, I don't believe there was any of that. It would come as a surprise to me if it was. I think, after all, you would not wish to go into a Dental Reference practice in any way prejudiced. You want to go in with an open mind and you need to see things as they are, not from what you have read.

Lord Leon Brittan (1939-2015): "A German Jew." Lord Denning (1899-1999).

NINE: GDC Chambers, November 18, 2008:

ANDREW HURST (BARRISTER THAT WAS INSTRUCTED BY THE GDC): It was a bad question because there were two questions in one, so perhaps I ought to go back and break it down. First of all, did you provide the previous reports of your visits in advance of the practice inspection in February?

RICHARD HILL (NHS): I'm not aware of them being provided for that purpose.

ANDREW HURST (BARRISTER THAT WAS INSTRUCTED BY THE GDC): Well, again, is it that you provided them and then we can discuss what the reason was?

RICHARD HILL (NHS): They were provided but then, again, they would be within the practitioner's file so there would be ready access to them.

ANDREW HURST (BARRISTER THAT WAS INSTRUCTED BY THE GDC): So you did provide them but for the purpose—

RICHARD HILL (NHS): Indirectly, I would say. I do not recall whatsoever being asked to do so for the purpose of the visit.

THE CHAIRMAN (DR SHIV PABARY, MBE, JP): I think what is trying to be established is did you provide them or are you saying that the PCT would have had access to them anyway?

RICHARD HILL (NHS): Yes, the PCT would have access.

THE CHAIRMAN (DR SHIV PABARY, MBE JP): So the PCT could have provided them.

RICHARD HILL (NHS): That's right. They would have access to them.

THE CHAIRMAN (DR SHIV PABARY, MBE JP): The question was did you provide them specifically.

RICHARD HILL (NHS): For that purpose?

THE CHAIRMAN (DR SHIV PABARY, MBE JP): Yes.

RICHARD HILL (NHS): No, is the answer to that.

THE CHAIRMAN (DR SHIV PABARY, MBE JP): Not for that purpose, did you provide them at all? Were you asked for them?

RICHARD HILL (NHS): I provided all inspection sheets previously, but not for that purpose—well, as a matter of routine. I mean, part of the reason why we do so was obviously because there was going to be a Health Care Commission inspection or visit to the PCT which is done on a regular basis. But I was not aware of those being passed to the Dental Reference Officer. They may have been, I don't know, but I was not aware of that.

NEGRO'S PERSPECTIVE:

They were all pure white, and their INDIAN was in a very, very, very, advanced stage in the metamorphosis of becoming PURE WHITE (PUPA), and their Coconut Dalit was whiter inside, and they lied, and lied, and lied again— like a French Bulletin, and they lied that they did not lie – **Psalm 144.**

"The highest reach of injustice is to be deemed just when you are not." Plato.

Then, verdicts were prior agreed in ANTICHRIST FREEMASONS' TEMPLES, and in open courts, incompetent art incompetently imitated life – **Habakkuk 1:4.**

"The white man is the devil." Elijah Mohammed (1897-1975).

Negrophobic Perjury guarded Persecutory Negrophobia: Based on cogent irrefutable, and available evidence, crooked, hereditary RACIST, and pure white bastard, Richard Hill, unrelentingly lied under oath and on record, and his pure white kindred, and their INDIAN, the near perfect imitation of the pure white higher upper-class Englishman—knew or ought to know that their own pure white kindred lied when he stated: "I don't think so, no. I think that's a wrong reading of it. I don't think that we did anything of the sort. I don't think she read any of those—in my knowledge, according to my knowledge, I don't believe there was any of that. It would come as a surprise to me if it was. I think, after all, you would not wish to go into a Dental Reference practice in any way prejudiced. You want to go in with an open mind and you need to see things as they are, not from what you have read."

Creeping DPRK.

Leviticus 19: 33–34: They kill foreigners, only foreigners.

Their type killed the NIGERIAN, only 56, and the INDIAN, only 42, albeit hands-off, with the mens rea hidden in the belly of the actus reus.

Google: Dr Richard Bamgboye, GP.

Google: Dr Anand Kamath, Dentist.

OYINBO OLE/ODE: Based on cogent irrefutable, and available evidence, crooked, hereditary RACIST, and pure white bastard, Richard Hill, unrelentingly lied under oath and on record, and his pure white kindred, and their

INDIAN, the near perfect imitation of the pure white higher upper-class Englishman—knew or ought to know that their own pure white kindred lied when he stated: "I'm not aware of them being provided for that purpose."

ANDREW HURST, OUR ENGLAND'S CLASS SENIOR JUDGE OF OUR EMPIRE OF STOLEN INHERITANCE—HABAKKUK: If there are cogent and irrefutable evidence that the pure white ancestors of your own pure white father and mother were THIEVES, merciless racist murderers, and owners of stolen children of defenceless poor people, it would be very, very, very, naive not to expect RACIAL HATRED guarded by incompetent mendacity to be part of your own genetic inheritances: Persecutory Negrophobia guarded by Negrophobic Perjury—**Habakkuk 1:4.** A crooked hereditary RACIST pure white bastard ultra-righteously sat on the BONES of stolen children of defenceless poor people , future flats and absolutely inevitable distant future's NUCLEAR ASH, and Judged Sinners—**John 8:7, Matthew 7:1–6.** RACIST descendants of murderers, THIEVES, and owners of stolen children of defenceless poor AFRICANS, blue-eyed demons, do not have the MORAL RIGHT to Judge sinners.

Google: The White Judge Lied. Google: Mediocre GDC.

"Blue-eyed devils." Elijah Mohammed (1897–1975).

Matthew 12:27: Blue-eyed devils cannot cast out green-eyed demons.

"Who am I to Judge?" Pope Francis (1936–2025). No one is good, not even one—**Psalm 53**, but God Almighty Judges no one—**John 5:22.**

ANDREW HURST: A brainless scatter-head pure white rubbish, having FAILED in practice, loads did, he parked his liability at public till.

One of the reasons why the GDP of the USA is about 10X bigger than that of the UK (>$30 trillion: >$3 trillion <$4 trillion) is that scatter-head, hereditary RACIST, and crooked pure white bastards are paid the salary of Senior Judges (>£250K/Annum).

Based on cogent irrefutable, and available evidence, crooked, hereditary RACIST, and pure white bastard, Richard Hill, unrelentingly lied under oath and on record, and his pure white kindred, and their INDIAN, the near perfect imitation of the pure white higher upper-class Englishman—knew or ought to know that their own pure white kindred lied when he stated: "They were provided but then, again, they would be within the practitioner's file so there would be ready access to them."

ANDREW HURST, OUR SENIOR JUDGE, ALBEIT ENGLAND'S CLASS: It is not the TRUTH that daily dialogues with pure white imbeciles (predominantly but not exclusively pure white) is a proper job that is worthwhile and manly—**Habakkuk 1:4.**

"They may not have been well written from a grammatical point of view but I am confident I had not forgotten any of the facts." Pure White, Crooked, and Hereditary Racist Welsh Imbecile.

OYINBO ODE: A PURE WHITE IMBECILE: ARCHIE IS IMPURE (<43% NIGERIAN).

ANDREW HURST, OUR SENIOR JUDGE, ALBEIT ENGLAND'S CLASS: Our own Nigeria, Shell's Docile Cash Cow since 1956. GDC was established in 1956. Our own MONEY, Nigeria (oil/gas) is by far more relevant to the economic survival of all your own mentally gentler white children, your own pure white mother, your pure white father, and your pure white spouse than Nick Griffin's Llanerfyl Powys.

OYINBO OLE/ODE: A RACIST DESCENDANT OF THIEVES HAS NO MORAL RIGHT TO JUDGE SINNERS—**John 8:7, Matthew 7:1–6.**

Based on cogent irrefutable, and available evidence, crooked, hereditary RACIST, and pure white bastard, Richard Hill, unrelentingly lied under oath and on record, and his pure white kindred, and their INDIAN, the near perfect imitation of the pure white higher upper-class Englishman—knew or ought to know that their own pure white kindred lied when he stated: "Indirectly, I would say. I do not recall whatsoever being asked to do so for the purpose of the visit."

Their Pakistani looking, physically ill-favoured, mentally wonky (probably incestuously conceived), crooked, and hereditary RACIST Coconut Dalit who seemed to impersonate a Maharajah—knew or ought to know that Richard Hill lied when he stated: "Yes, the PCT would have access."

ANDREW HURST, OUR ENGLAND'S CLASS SENIOR JUDGE OF OUR EMPIRE OF STOLEN INHERITANCE—HABAKKUK: Reasoning and vision do not have finite boundaries. The fellow is who He says He is—**John 14:6.** The supernatural exists and it is consistently accessible to those who stand where it can come—**John 14:26.** The mind that I did not choose is FINER than your unashamedly mediocre fish and chips JUSTICE SYSTEM, and I do not believe in any part of SHIT, as no part of SHIT is good, not even one—Psalm 53, and I have the POWER to use cogent facts and irrefutable evidence to irreparably destroy you and every part of SHIT—**Habakkuk 1:4.**

ANDREW HURST, OUR ENGLAND'S CLASS SENIOR JUDGE OF OUR EMPIRE OF STOLEN INHERITANCE—**HABAKKUK:** The pure white ancestors of your own pure white father and mother were

THIEVES—**Habakkuk:** Extremely nasty and merciless RACIST MURDERERS, nastier than Yevgeny Prigozhin (1961–2023), and Hitler (1889–1945), several years of NAZI HOLOCAUST (1939–1945) was a mere storm in a teacup compared to MAAFA (1445–1888), industrial-scale professional armed robbers, armed land grabbers, gun runners, drug dealers (opium merchants of the Qing Dynasty), and owners of stolen children of defenceless poor AFRICANS.

Their Pakistani looking, physically ill-favoured, mentally wonky (probably incestuously conceived), crooked, and hereditary RACIST Coconut Dalit who seemed to impersonate a Maharajah—knew or ought to know that Richard Hill lied when he stated: "That's right. They would have access to them."

Based on several decades of very, very, very, proximate observations and direct experiences, their unashamedly MEDIOCRE Fish and Chips Justice System is irreparably FU*KED, it has foreseeably succumbed to INCEST, weakening of the common genetic pool, and associated physical and/or mental wonkiness, and hereditary white supremacist Freemason Judges, and others, who make loads of MONEY from unashamed mediocrity and confusion PROP SHIT UP: Conflict of interest.

"A government that robs Peter to pay Paul can always depend on the support of Paul." George Bernard Shaw (1856–1950).

Their Pakistani looking, physically ill-favoured, mentally wonky (probably incestuously conceived), crooked, and hereditary RACIST Coconut Dalit who seemed to impersonate a Maharajah—knew or ought to know that Richard Hill lied when he stated: "I provided all inspection sheets previously, but not for that purpose—well, as a matter of routine. I mean, part of the reason why we do so was obviously because there was going to be a Health Care Commission inspection or visit to the PCT which is done on a regular basis. But I was not aware of those being passed to the Dental Reference Officer. They may have been, I don't know, but I was not aware of that."

They do not want their own mentally gentler white children (OECD) and the PURE WHITE IMBECILES they shepherd (predominantly but not exclusively pure white) to know the TRUTH which is that apart from our INFERIOR SKIN COLOUR, and our INFERIOR ACCENT of speaking a foreign language, own people (AFRICANS) are also properly created by ALMIGHTY GOD, to conceal the truth, which is that our people (AFRICANS) are human beings too, members of their brainlessly and baselessly self-awarded SUPERIOR RACE criminally steal yields of our own people's Christ-granted talents, secure in the knowledge that all JUDGES would be PURE WHITE, and their hope is that they would be hereditary RACIST PURE WHITE BASTARDS TOO—**Habakkuk 1:4.** The poor pure white ancestors of his pure white father and mother were incompetent RACIST LIARS too, like the pure white ancestors of King's School and Oxbridge-educated Lord Justice Charles Anthony Haddon-Cave, KC, a RACIST son of a very, very, very, RICH Tasmanian Colonialist Economic Cannibal (**Mark 10:25**), Sir Charles Phillip Haddon-Cave (1925–1999), and an impostor and an expert of deception (perception is grander than reality), and a closeted hereditary white supremacist descendant of DRUG LORDS (Opium Merchants of the Qing Dynasty), and a homie of Eton and Oxbridge-educated rich men's son (**Mark 10:25**), Archbishop Justin Welby, they were THIEVES and owners of stolen children of defenceless poor people, including the pure black African ancestors of our IMPURE DUCHESS OF SUSSEX, Princess Ada Mazi Omu of Arochukwu, Princess Meghan Markle (43%

Nigerian), and her impure children (<43% Nigerian)—**Habakkuk.**

A very, very, very, very, DISHONEST typical pure white Englishman. A crooked closeted hereditary racist Freemason.

"He is a typical Englishman, usually violent and always dull." Wilde (1854–1900).

"Could you take on the RUSSIANS by yourselves." President Trump

"England will fight to the last American." American saying

1944: There were >1 million American Soldiers in Great Britain, including hundreds of thousands of Black American soldiers.

"Ethical foreign policy." Brother Robin Cook (1946–2005).

Psalm 118:22, Luke 20:17: If BROTHER BUILDERS are as ethical and as brave as they brag, they must use extreme overwhelming violence to evict PUTIN from Crimea. PUTIN used extreme overwhelming violence to convert Bakhmut from bricks to rubble and stole it—**Exodus 20:15.**

Flat track bullies. Trump's poodles: Their hairs stand on end when they are challenged by AFRICANS, we and our type are the ones hereditary RACIST pure white bastards (predominantly but not exclusively pure white) would beat up without the support of the YANKS. The YANKS are NATO, and absolutely everything else is an auxiliary bluff.

Mark 10:25: Elon Musk: Hereditary Intra-Racial Sex Machine.

TEN: John 14:26: When the DIVINE HELPER unravels Merciless Hereditary RACIAL HATRED, to save face, Members of their Brainlessly and Baselessly Self-awarded SUPERIOR RACE unleash their EVIL RACIST THUNDER: The Lunatic Negro Card. Any NEGRO who disagrees with any member of their Brainlessly and Baselessly Self-awarded SUPERIOR RACE—is mental.

"He has refused to submit to a medical examination." King's School and Oxbridge-educated Lord Justice Charles Anthony Haddon-Cave, KC, a RACIST son of a very, very, very, RICH Tasmanian Colonialist Economic Cannibal (**Mark 10:25**), Sir Charles Phillip Haddon-Cave (1925–1999), an impostor and an expert of deception (perception is grander than reality), and a closeted hereditary white supremacist descendant of DRUG LORDS (Opium Merchants of the Qing Dynasty), and a homie of Eton and Oxbridge-educated rich men's son (**Mark 10:25**), Archbishop Justin Welby.

BRAINLESS RACIST NONSENSE. GOOGLE: THE WHITE JUDGE LIED.

"To disagree with three-fourths of the British public on all points is one of the first requisites of sanity, one of the deepest consolations in all moments of spiritual doubt." Wilde (1854–1900).

They hate our own people (AFRICANS), and we know, and they hate our children more, but they don't know. Based on several decades of very, very, very, proximate observations and direct experiences, the only part of AFRICA that hereditary RACIST pure white bastards (predominantly but not exclusively pure white) truly love is our own money, our own AFRICA'S NATURAL RESOURCES, and absolutely everything else is DECEIT.

"How Europe underdeveloped Africa." Dr Walter Rodney (1942–1980).

Then, very, very, very, greedy armed hunters of men, and those they armed, carried and sold millions of stolen children of defenceless poor people, now THIEVES steal our own natural resources from our own AFRICA - **Habakkuk.**

SUBSTITUTION IS FRAUDULENT EMANCIPATION.

"Moderation is a virtue only among those who are thought to have found alternatives." Dr Henry Kissinger (1923–2023).

Facts are sacred and cannot be overstated: "Find the truth and tell it." Harold Pinter (1930-2008).

Based on several decades of very, very, proximate observations and direct experiences, they LIED to their own mentally gentler WHITE CHILDREN (OECD) and the pure white imbeciles they shepherd (predominantly but not exclusively pure white) that they are ULTRA-RIGHTEOUS GENIUSES, very, very, very, highly civilised, and super-enlightened, and they do everything LEGALLY: Rules-based procedures, precedent, and statute etcetera, and including RACIAL HATRED and FRAUD—**Habakkuk 1:4.**

****

GDC CHAMBERS, 18.11.2008:

ANDREW HURST (BARRISTER THAT WAS INSTRUCTED BY THE GDC): So you are not aware of the reason, but you did provide—

RICHARD HILL (NHS): No, but they were provided as part of the routine monitoring, that's all. But, as I said, they might have been shown to the Dental Reference Officer. I'm not aware of it.

ANDREW HURST (BARRISTER THAT WAS INSTRUCTED BY THE GDC): We can ask her later.

RICHARD HILL (NHS): It's not a matter that I actually discussed with her either.

ANDREW HURST (BARRISTER THAT WAS INSTRUCTED BY THE GDC): Thank you. Now obviously during the course of the run up to the visit of 22 February there was some communication between you and Stephanie Twidale.

RICHARD HILL (NHS): Yes.

NEGRO'S PERSPECTIVE:

Dr Richard Hill (NHS) implied that the only way that Dr Stephanie Twidale (TD) could know about the reports of 22.07.2004 and follow up an undisclosed date, which he extraordinarily created from handwritten drafts, which recorded other matters was if she saw and read the reports. He talked rot. Those regularly spun are amongst the least literate and numerate in the industrialised world.

"I don't think so, no. I think that's a wrong reading of it. I don't think that we did anything of the sort. I don't think she read any of those—in my knowledge, according to my knowledge, I don't believe there was any of that. It would come as a surprise to me if it was. I think, after all, you would not wish to go into a Dental Reference practice in any way prejudiced. You want to go in with an open mind and you need to see things as they are, not from what you have read. Dr Richard Hill (NHS)

So, according to Dr Richard Hill (NHS), if Dr Stephen Twidale (TD) had seen and read, and/or been told about the created reports of 22.07.2004 and follow up of undisclosed date, it would have prejudiced and compromised her inspection of 22.02.2007.

There are only four sentences in the created reports of 22.07.2004 and follow up of an undisclosed date; all of them are founded upon impossible deduction—certum quia impossibile est.

It is indisputable and irrefutable that Dr Stephanie Twidale (TD) asked to see reports prior to visiting, and it is the absolute truth that she was given Dr Richard Hill's (NHS) contact details, and he was asked to expect to hear from her.

"Richard, Stephanie Twidale called us a few weeks ago about DRS visits and Charlotte prioritised Mr Bamgbelu's practice; Stephanie has been in touch a few times as her colleagues had highlighted issues from a similar practice in Northants and they would like to review report etc etc prior to visiting. She also wanted to know if there has been a dental inspection there at all and I did not know the answer.... Cue Richard have you carried out an inspection at this practice, please could you advise Stephanie when she contacts you, and would it be possible to see our reports so we can be more proactive with any other queries. Thanks. With kind Regards, John Hooper (NHS), 15.08.2006

They were all PURE WHITE: Homogeneity in the administration of their law is an impregnable secure mask of merciless RACIST EVIL, an intelligently designed WEAPON OF RACE WAR.

Based on cogent, irrefutable, and available evidence, it is the TRUTH that about three weeks later (15.08.2006–06.09.2006), Dr Richard Hill (NHS) released the reports of 22.07.2004 and follow up of undisclosed date, which he extraordinarily forged from handwritten drafts, which recorded other matters. The reports were abruptly withdrawn on 16.10.2008, more than four years after the alleged visit of 22.07.2004.

"The pure white man is the devil." Brother Khalid Mohammed (1948–2001) paraphrased.

'Last white couple in a Leicester street reveal how the community has changed over 40 years.'

Grey Squirrels versus Red Squirrels: The demographic war is absolutely unwinnable, and reverse colonisation is absolutely unstoppable. Facts are sacred and cannot be overstated.

OYINBO ODE: "The best opportunity of developing academically and emotional." Our own Mediocre, Wonky, Pure White Hereditary Racist, unashamedly functionally semi-illiterate, poly-educated poor man's son, a mere former debt-collector Solicitor in Norfolk/Norwich (5th Rate Partner), and the Senior Vice President of the Association of Her Majesty's District Judges, Bedford's District Judge Paul Robert Ayers, 3, St Paul's Square, MK 40 1SQ.

A brainless hereditary RACIST pure white bastard approved what his pure white father and mother spoke, which his poly-educated pure white superiors and supervisors in LUTON authorised. If the opportunist RACIST lowlife pure white rubbish read his approved Judgement, he was a FOOL, and if he did not, he lied as he implied that he did—**Habakkuk 1:4.** The poor pure white ancestors of his pure white father and mother were incompetent RACIST LIARS too, like the pure white ancestors of King's School and Oxbridge-educated Lord Justice Charles Anthony Haddon-Cave, KC, a RACIST son of a very, very, very, RICH Tasmanian Colonialist Economic Cannibal (**Mark 10:25**), Sir Charles Phillip Haddon-Cave (1925–1999), and an impostor and an expert of deception, and a closeted hereditary white supremacist descendant of DRUG LORDS (Opium

Merchants of the Qing Dynasty), and a homie of Eton and Oxbridge-educated rich men's son (**Mark 10:25**), Archbishop Justin Welby, they were THIEVES and owners of stolen children of defenceless poor people, including the pure black African ancestors of our IMPURE DUCHESS OF SUSSEX, Princess Ada Mazi Omu of Arochukwu, Princess Meghan Markle (43% Nigerian), and her impure children (<43% Nigerian)—**Habakkuk**.

BEDFORD,ENGLAND: Our own Mediocre, Wonky, Pure White Hereditary Racist, unashamedly functionally semi-illiterate, poly-educated poor man's son, a mere former debt-collector Solicitor in Norfolk/Norwich (5th Rate Partner), and the Senior Vice President of the Association of Her Majesty's District Judges, Bedford's District Judge Paul Robert Ayers, 3, St Paul's Square, MK 40 1SQ, in our own NIGERIA, our own NIGERIAN BABIES with huge oil wells and gas fields near their huts eat only 1.5/day in our own NIGERIA, a very, very, very, hereditary RACIST pure white bastard, a mere poly-educated former debt-collector Solicitor in bland and colourless NORFOLK/NORWICH (Coastal Dole/the Departure Lounge of Life), lowlife 5th Rate Partner—whose pure white father and mother have never seen CRUDE OIL, and whose pure white ancestors, including the pure white ancestors of ANEURIN BEVAN (1897–1960), and DAME MARGARET SEWARD (1935–2021), were fed like battery hens with huge yields of millions of stolen children of defenceless poor people , was our Senior District Judge in BEDFORD, Great Britain. Which part of our own shithole Africa is GREAT?

BEDFORD,ENGLAND: Our own Mediocre, Wonky, Pure White Hereditary Racist, unashamedly functionally semi-illiterate, poly-educated poor man's son, a mere former debt-collector Solicitor in Norfolk/Norwich (5th Rate Partner), and the Senior Vice President of the Association of Her Majesty's District Judges, Bedford's District Judge Paul

Robert Ayers, 3, St Paul's Square, MK 40 1SQ, our ultra-righteous hereditary RACIST pure white bastard DISHONESTLY implied that he did not know that the pure white ancestors of his pure white father and mother were THIEVES, extremely nasty RACIST MURDERERS, and owners of stolen children of defenceless poor people, including the pure black African ancestors of our IMPURE DUCHESS OF SUSSEX, Princess Ada Mazi Omu of Arochukwu, Princess Meghan Markle (43% Nigerian), and her impure children (<43% Nigerian)—**Habakkuk.**

BEDFORD,ENGLAND: Our own Mediocre, Wonky, Pure White Hereditary Racist, unashamedly functionally semi-illiterate, poly-educated poor man's son, a mere former debt-collector Solicitor in Norfolk/Norwich (5th Rate Partner), and the Senior Vice President of the Association of Her Majesty's District Judges, Bedford's District Judge Paul Robert Ayers, 3, St Paul's Square, MK 40 1SQ, our ignorant descendant armed robbers and opium merchants (**Habakkuk**), also dishonestly implied that he did not know that SLAVERY rebuilt everything it succeeded and paid for everything it preceded, including ANEURIN BEVAN'S NHS (1948), and DAME MARGARET SEWARD'S GDC (1956).

BEDFORD,ENGLAND: Our own Mediocre, Wonky, Pure White Hereditary Racist, unashamedly functionally semi-illiterate, poly-educated poor man's son, a mere former debt-collector Solicitor in Norfolk/Norwich (5th Rate Partner), and the Senior Vice President of the Association of Her Majesty's District Judges, Bedford's District Judge Paul Robert Ayers, 3, St Paul's Square, MK 40 1SQ, our properly schooled impostor and an expert of deception further LIED when he dishonestly implied that he did not know that equitable, fair, and just REPARATION pends, and several centuries of unpaid interest accrue.

"Record of Practice Visits-Bedford PCT. Dear John, Please find attached the record of practice visits that you were chasing up. Sorry for the delay! As you can see, the great majority of practices are not a cause for concern. However, we will need to focus particularly on the Bamgbelu and the alpha practices. Perhaps also beta practice in delta and the gamma practice are worthy of closer attention. Regards, Richard. (NHS email of 06.09.2006)

"RECORD OF PRACTICE VISITS: BEDFORD PCT. DENTIST: Mr O Bamgbelu. ADDRESS: Grey Friars Dental Practice 52 Bromham Road Bedford MK40 2QG. Telephone No: 01234300505. Visit Date: JULY 2004. CONCERNS: No risk assessment, no CoSSH, A Kavoclave type autoclave was present in the surgery. This type of autoclave should not be used as the cycle can be broken into before sterilisation is complete. No other member of staff were present at the visit so could not be questioned as regards the methods of cross infection control used by practice. (NHS report of 22.07.2004)

OUTSTANDING ISSUES: Even though the necessary documents have now been seen. I continue to have concerns as to the cross infection control procedures in the practice. (NHS report of undisclosed date)

The incompetently criminally fabricated NHS reports were withdrawn - in toto, on 16.10.2008, more than four years after the alleged visit of 22.07.2004.

"The white man was created a devil, to bring chaos upon the earth." Malcom X (1925–1965).

OYINBO OLE/ODE: Mark Fuhrman (LAPD) and Richard Hill (NHS) are PURE WHITE, but Archie is IMPURE (<43% Nigerian).

Prior to the withdrawal of the incompetently criminally fabricated NHS report of July 22, 2004, and its follow up of undisclosed date, Dr Stephanie Twidale (TD) had several discussions with the NHS about the reports that Dr Richard hill (NHS) created for her. If a crooked and hereditary RACIST pure white woman read the news or listened to it and/or watched it on the television, why should the news be different if she heard it on the radio?

OCCULTIST HEREDITARY WHITE SUPREMACIST BASTARDS: Their people are everywhere, and they control almost everything, including RACIAL HATRED and FRAUD—Habakkuk 1:4. Integrity, friendship, respect, and charity: All for one, and one for all.

There is no evidence that Mr David Morris (MPS barrister), Dr Shiv Pabary (MBE, JP) and Dr Richard Hill (MBE) were members of the unelected (illegal, parallel power), not merit Based and a closet racist: a satanic network, but extraordinarily they all placed significant emphasis on Dr Stephanie Twidale (TD) seeing the incompetently fabricated Racist NHS Reports, and implied that if she heard about the four sentences—report, as long as she did not see them, she could not know about them.

'Attila, the scourge of God, the French, his brothers.' Italian saying

They lied like a French bulletin. 'He lies like a French bulletin.' Dutch saying

Those regularly spun are amongst the least literate and numerate in the industrialised world. Pure White, Crooked, and Hereditary Racist BRITISH SOLDIER, Dr Stephanie Twidale (TD), may the French ulcer love your four-fifth deflated very, very, very, ugly looking mammary gland (only one of the two ugly lumps of tissues that lay on your pectoralis major), with NO MILK, not a single drop milk, but plenty of blood. You were so ugly, you must have been a LIBIDO KILLER at your starting, at your bloom.

"Truth, Sir, is the cow that will yield such people no more milk, so they are gone to milk the bull." Dr Samuel Johnson (1709–1784).

Pure White, Crooked, and Hereditary Racist BRITISH SOLDIER, Dr Stephanie Twidale (TD), 'May the French ulcer love you and the Lord hate you.' An Arabian curse

'Having discussed with the PCT they told me that Mr Hill had made previous visits not that long before from which there had been some queries, and they felt perhaps it would be sensible for Mr Hill to come along as well with me to be a second person and follow up on his previous visits to the practice.' Stephanie Twidale (TD)

'I spoke to Dr Sue Gregory, Consultant in Dental Public Health at the Bedfordshire PCT to impart the information and was informed that Richard Hill, Dental Practice adviser to Bedfordshire PCT, had carried out a previous Surgery inspection at Bromham Road that had raised some concerns.' Stephanie Twidale (TD)

'Then I know it came through that Richard Hill had been in before about 6 months ago, I think they said, and it was probably sensible for him to go as the second person, a second appropriate second person to do a follow up. The actual timings of bits of those I am afraid I can't REMEMBER.' Stephanie Twidale (TD)

'Dear Stephanie, Just to confirm that I have spoken with Richard Hill and he will join you for the DRS visit on Thursday 22nd February to Mr Bamgbelu's Bedford Practice, commencing at 9 am. We will endeavour to share any issues that the PCT may have with you PRIOR to the 22nd. Kind regards, Sue.' Sue Gregory (OBE)

Their case against the NEGRO was DESTROYED by the DIVINE HELPER—**John 14:26,** but the desire for lawyers to make money kept it alive.

"The one great principle of English law is, to make business for itself." Charles Dicken (1812-1870).

****

GDC CHAMBERS, 19.11.2008: DAVID MORRIS (BARRISTER THAT WAS INSTRUCTED BY THE MPS): This is a report by Richard Hill dated 22 July 2004. Might you have seen that before the inspection?

STEPHANIE TWIDALE (TD): No, I have never seen this before.

DAVID MORRIS (BARRISTER THAT WAS INSTRUCTED BY THE MPS): Sir, you will recall Mr Hill's evidence was that this is a report mistakenly attributed to Mr Bamgbelu's practice when it in fact relates to something that was a mistake?

THE CHAIRMAN (DR SHIV PABARY, MBE, JP): Was this where there was a lot of cancellations? I remember something in evidence.

DAVID MORRIS (BARRISTER THAT WAS INSTRUCTED BY THE MPS): Mr Hill said yesterday that while he made an error and he thought there had been an inspection on 22 July 2004, and in fact that was not right, it referred to another practice. In chatting with Richard Hill, presumably you did before going round, did he mention any previous inspections that he had done?

STEPHANIE TWIDALE (TD): I never spoke to Richard Hill, nor had I ever met him before we arrived at the practice together. It was a classic two people standing outside a building saying: 'Are you? Oh yes, right fine' we had never met and we did not speak beforehand. The only people I spoke to beforehand would be John Hooper and some e-mail correspondence with John, with Charlotte Dowling and with the Consultants in public health, Sue Gregory. I didn't actually have any contact with Richard at all.

NEGRO'S PERSPECTIVE:

"Was this where there was a lot of cancellations? I remember something in evidence." Shiv Pabary (MBE), Crooked, Hereditary Racist, physically ill-favoured, and mentally wonky, and Scatter-head Coconut Dalit, albeit Member of the Most Excellent Order of our Empire of Stolen Inheritance—**Habakkuk.**

BLAME EVERYTHING ON INCEST: NORTHERN, ENGLAND, THE SERENGETI OF INCESTUOUSLY CONCEIVED PHYSICALLY AND/OR MENTALLY WONKY BROWN BASTARDS.

Lord Leon Brittan (1939-2015): "A German Jew." Lord Denning (1899-1999).

ELEVEN: Everything Shiv Pabary (MBE), our Crooked, Hereditary Racist, physically ill-favoured, mentally wonky, and Scatter-head Coconut Dalit, albeit Member of the Most Excellent Order of our Empire of Stolen Inheritance—**Habakkuk,** could remember was a lie, and everything the properly schooled impostor and an expert of deception (perception is always grander than reality) could not remember—was the TRUTH.

As vision and reasoning is infinite, there is no riddle that could not be unravelled, or could withstand the bombardment of persistent reasoning—using only accurate facts. Stephanie Twidale (TD) sowed the seed of confusion with the full knowledge of David Morris (MPS barrister). Dr Shiv Pabary (MBE, JP) corroborated the 'see' and 'read' racist trickery, which seemed to have been agreed in secret. The plan seemed perfect in secret, but it was brainless in the open. To read the report, Dr Stephanie Twidale (TD) must see it, but it is possible to know about the reports (only four sentences) without seeing and reading it, as she admitted that she had several discussions with the NHS about them.

****

GDC CHAMBERS, 19.11.2008: THE CHAIRMAN (DR SHIV PABARY, MBE, JP): Just to clarify that, prior to your visit to Mr Bamgbelu's practice you had not seen any practice visit reports?

STEPHANIE TWIDALE (TD): Nothing at all.

THE CHAIRMAN (DR SHIV PABARY, MBE, JP): Nor had you had discussions with Mr Hill about any concerns?

STEPHANIE TWIDALE (TD): Nothing at all, nothing at all. We would normally as a Reference Officer try and work in that way if at all possible.

THE CHAIRMAN (DR SHIV PABARY, MBE, JP): Thank you.

***

NEGRO'S PERSPECTIVE:

Our Crooked, Hereditary Racist, physically ill-favoured, mentally wonky, and Scatter-head Coconut Dalit, albeit Member of the Most Excellent Order of our Empire of Stolen Inheritance—**Habakkuk,** Justice of Peace (JP), and the archetypal GDC Committee Chairperson, implied that the only way that Dr Stephanie Twidale (TD) could know about previous reports that she sought was if she saw them, or the creator of the fabricated NHS reports confesses that he discussed them with her. Really!

BRAINLESS RACIST NONSENSE: BLAME IT ALL ON INCEST.

'Nor had you had discussions with Mr Hill about any concerns?' Dr Shiv Pabary, MBE, JP

If Dr Stephanie Twidale (TD) had stated under oath that she had never met and had never spoken to Dr Richard Hill, and further stated under oath that she did not have any contact with him (Dr Richard Hill, NHS), how could she have discussions with someone that she LIED that she did not have any contact with prior to the inspection of 22.02.2007?

BRAINLESS RACIST NONSENSE: A VERY, VERY, VERY, DULL COCONUT DALIT, SHIV PABARY

(MBE) REASONED LIKE SOMEONE WHOSE MUM AND DAD ARE COUSINS, LIKE CHARLES DARWIN'S CHILDREN. BLAME IT ALL ON INCEST.

'There is no sin except stupidity.' Wilde (1854–1900).

'I never spoke to Richard Hill, nor had I ever met him before we arrived at the practice together. It was a classic two people standing outside a building saying: "Are you? Oh yes, right fine" we had never met and we did not speak beforehand. The only people I spoke to beforehand would be John Hooper and some e-mail correspondence with John, with Charlotte Dowling and with the Consultants in public health, Sue Gregory. I didn't actually have any contact with Richard at all.' Dr Stephanie Twidale (TD)

If Dr Stephanie Twidale (TD) asked to review reports prior to visiting, and she was given Dr Richard Hill's (NHS) contact details on or before 15.08.2006, and in an email of 30.11.2006, Dr Sue Gregory stated that she had asked Richard Hill (NHS) to accompany Dr Stephanie Twidale (TD) to the inspection and he would she concerns with her, and more importantly, Dr Richard Hill (NHS) stated that he had contact with Dr Stephanie Twidale, it must mean that our Crooked, Hereditary Racist, physically ill-favoured, mentally wonky, and Scatter-head Coconut Dalit, albeit Member of the Most Excellent Order of our Empire of Stolen Inheritance—**Habakkuk,** Justice of Peace (JP), and the archetypal GDC Committee Chairperson was taking a quick nap when Dr Richard Hill (NHS) gave his testimony a day earlier (18.11.2008) or he was pathologically confused. Alzheimer's disease and Atypical Dementia are considerably more common than ordinarily realised.

Alzheimer's disease and Atypical Dementia are incompatible with the competent administration of English

Law. The competent administration of English Law should be an inviolable basic right.

The law seemed paralysed. It will be naivety that borders upon dishonesty to suggest that the general decline in educational standards has left any part of the society untouched.

****

GDC CHAMBERS, 18.11.2008: ANDREW HURST (GDC's barrister): Thank you. Now obviously during the course of the run up to the visit of 22 February there was some communication between you and Stephanie Twidale.

RICHARD HILL (NHS): Yes.

****

So, if Richard Hill (NHS), under oath, on 18.11.2008, told our Crooked, Hereditary Racist, physically ill-favoured, mentally wonky, and Scatter-head Coconut Dalit, albeit Member of the Most Excellent Order of our Empire of Stolen Inheritance—**Habakkuk**, Justice of Peace (JP), and the archetypal GDC Committee Chairperson that he had contact with Stephanie Twidale (TD) prior to 22.02.2007, and Stephanie Twidale (TD) said she didn't, why was theirs not a fish and chips legal process?

Our Crooked, Hereditary Racist, physically ill-favoured, mentally wonky, and Scatter-head Coconut Dalit, albeit Member of the Most Excellent Order of our Empire of Stolen Inheritance—**Habakkuk,** Justice of Peace (JP), and the archetypal GDC Committee Chairperson was intellectually very, very, very, soft; he was an actor, an impostor and an expert of deception. The crooked Dalit did not have the intellectual agility to do the job that he was asked to do.

If Dr Richard Hill (NHS) stated under oath that he kept reports in files within NHS offices, and these files were available to the NHS (PCT), and he told Dr Shiv Pabary (MBE, JP) that the PCT had access to the alleged files, why did Dr Shiv Pabary (MBE) imply that the only way Dr Stephanie Twidale (TD) could know about previous reports was if she physically saw them (only four sentences) or if Richard Hill (NHS) confessed that he directly discussed them with her?

KULI ODE: A VERY, VERY, VERY, DULL COCONUT DALIT, AND A PROPERLY SCHOOLED IMPOSTOR AND AN EXPERT OF DECEPTION (PERCEPTION IS ALWAYS GRANDER THAN REALITY)—**HABAKKUK 1:4.**

Shiv Pabary, our Crooked, Hereditary Racist, physically ill-favoured, mentally wonky (his mum and dad could be related), and Scatter-head Coconut Dalit, albeit Member of the Most Excellent Order of our Empire of Stolen Inheritance—**Habakkuk**, Justice of Peace (JP), and the archetypal GDC Committee Chairperson, let me tell you, the mind that the NIGERIAN, from shithole Africa, did not choose is FINER than your unashamedly MEDIOCRE Fish and Chips Justice System, and he does not believe in any part of PURIFIED SHIT, as no part of PURIFIED SHIT is good, not even one—**Psalm 53,** and he has the POWER to use cogent FACTS and irrefutable evidence to irreparably destroy you and every part of PURIFIED SHIT—**Habakkuk.**

"Jesus is the bedrock of my faith." HM (1926–2022).

Shiv Pabary, our Crooked, Hereditary Racist, physically ill-favoured, mentally wonky, and Scatter-head Coconut Dalit, albeit Member of the Most Excellent Order of our Empire of Stolen Inheritance—**Habakkuk**, Justice of Peace (JP), and the archetypal GDC Committee Chairperson, reasoning and vision do not have finite boundaries. The fellow is who He says He is—**John 14:6**. The SUPERNATURAL exists, and it is consistently accessible to those who stand where it can come – **John 14:26**.

If all the GURUS in INDIA could disprove the TRUTH, which is that Shiv Pabary, our Crooked, Hereditary Racist, physically ill-favoured, mentally wonky, and Scatter-head Coconut Dalit, albeit Member of the Most Excellent Order of our Empire of Stolen Inheritance—**Habakkuk,** Justice of Peace (JP), and the archetypal GDC Committee Chairperson, unrelentingly lied under oath and on record, they will confirm the belief of hundreds of millions of INDIANS, which is that **John 14:6** and **John 14:26**, the supernatural core of the Faith, are LIES.

Misleading statements under oath should be perjury, but seemingly not when a black man is the victim of the perjury. Negrophobic Perjury guards Persecutory Negrophobia.

UK justice system is racist, suggests one of Britain's only …

https://www.independent.co.uk › UK › Home News

10 Jan 2017—At the same event, Mr Herbert also suggested ethnic minorities "should not place their faith in a justice system that had not been designed …

Rather than lose in a debate to a black man, they cheat. Their idea of a black man is the Afro Caribbean whose genes had endured centuries of reversed unnatural selection on cane and cotton plantations.

In 2005, Mr Bamgbelu's Wellingborough Practice was inspected, and he was essentially asked to provide paper work. Mr Bamgbelu fully and promptly acceded to the requests, and the issues were fully resolved and signed off in 2005. In the summer of 2006, Stephanie Twidale (TD) contacted Bedford NHS, and she informed it about the inspection at Mr Bamgbelu's Wellingborough surgery in 2005. She wanted to know whether Mr Bamgbelu practice had been inspected before, and desired to review report prior to visiting his surgery on 22.02.2007.

They were a properly organised gang of racist pure white bastards. Even Hitler would not admit to being a RACIST.

Luke 11:52: Like the Pharisees, they know their system; a lot of things are done off record.

Bedford NHS asked RICHARD HILL (NHS) for reports. He did not have any, and they did not have any, so he was implicitly asked to create some, with the tacit approval of Sue Gregory (OBE). He could have visited Mr Bamgbelu's practice then, but he chose to create reports for him, as the decision to get rid of the first ever and only black dentist in Bedford seemed set in stone, and they do not want to be seen to be directly involved with MERCILESS RACIST EVIL – **Habakkuk 1:4.**

"The white man is the devil." Elijah Mohammed (1897-1975).

Mr Bamgbelu was the first ever and only black dentist in Bedford and Wellingborough. Dr Richard Hill (NHS), retrospectively, chose a date (22.07.2004), which suited his own practice diary, a day that he was not working at his own practice. So, he retrospectively chose 22.07.2004 as the date that he visited Mr Bamgbelu's practice.

RICHARD HILL (NHS), a closet racist thug (white skin but a seemingly dark black brain) gambled, recklessly, that Mr Bamgbelu would be at work on 22.07.2004, or even if he was not, he would be in the country. Since his retrospectively created report of 22.07.2004 was created for a stereotypically dirty black man (white and Asian people did the cleaning; the black man paid for their services), but BLACKS are not only physically dirty, but they are also MORALLY DIRTIER, so the fabricated NHS RACIST REPORT was laden with cross infection issues, and for this reason, RICHARD HILL (NHS) created an implied follow up visit, but he did not attach a date to the implied follow up visit, as the probability of getting the two dates wrong would double, and the notion of 'falsus in uno falsus in omnibus' could apply, so he left the implied follow up visit of the cross infection issues laden visit of 22.07.2004 undated, and to further tie up the loose ends that he perceived, as implicitly instructed by SUE GREGORY (OBE), he stated that there was no other person at the alleged visit—making verification—his words against mine. Only stupid AFRICANS expect pure white Freemason Judges to measure their own pure white kindred with same yardstick they use to measure BLACKS.

"Record of Practice Visits-Bedford PCT. Dear John, Please find attached the record of practice visits that you were chasing up. Sorry for the delay! As you can see, the great majority of practices are not a cause for concern. However, we will need to focus particularly on the Bamgbelu and the alpha practices. Perhaps also beta practice in delta and the gamma practice are worthy of closer attention. Regards, Richard. NHS, 06.09.2006

RECORD OF PRACTICE VISITS: BEDFORD PCT. DENTIST: Mr O Bamgbelu. ADDRESS: Grey Friars Dental Practice 52 Bromham Road Bedford MK40 2QG. Telephone No: 01234300505. Visit Date: JULY 2004.

CONCERNS: No risk assessment, no CoSSH, A Kavoclave type autoclave was present in the surgery. This type of autoclave should not be used as the cycle can be broken into before sterilisation is complete. No other member of staff were present at the visit so could not be questioned as regards the methods of cross infection control used by practice. NHS REPORT OF 22.07.2004

OUTSTANDING ISSUES: Even though the necessary documents have now been seen. I continue to have concerns as to the cross infection control procedures in the practice. NHS REPORT OF UNDISCLOSED DATE

The Criminally Fabricated NHS Racist Reports were published and disseminated among the RACIST pure white bastards who commissioned the MERCILESS RACIST EVIL. Sue Gregory (OBE), the cardinal of merciless, destructive, racially biased confusion, and Charlotte Dowling Goodson (NHS) had the 'meat' that they desired, which they ordered or had been requesting Richard Hill (NHS) to forge or fabricate, on their table. So, they set about work. Stephanie Twidale, a very, very, very, distinguished Territorial Army officer (TD), and a GONG HUNTER, was to disambiguate, authenticate, and corroborate the incompetent, retrospective racist fabrications of 22.07.2004 and follow up of undisclosed date, all under the watch of Sue Gregory, Officer of the Most Excellent Order of our Empire of Stolen Inheritance - **Habakkuk**. Stephanie Twidale (TD) was to amalgamate the NHS's retrospective fabrications of 22.07.2004 and its successor, the follow up of undisclosed date with the inspection of 22.02.2007.

"The white was created a devil, to bring chaos upon the earth." Malcolm X (1925-1965).

Only two months after the inspection of 22.02.2007, on 27.04.2007, Mr Bamgbelu was given a notice of termination, and three months later, on 27.07.2007, Mr Bamgbelu's contract was terminated.

BEDFORD, ENGLAND: District Judge Paul Robert Ayers, a brainless hereditary RACIST pure white bastard was granted the platform to display HEREDITARY PREJUDICE: No brain. Poor natural resources. Several continuous centuries of STEALING and SLAVERY preceded their huge stolen inheritance – **Habakkuk**.

New Herod, **Matthew 2:16:** They deceive their own mentally gentler white children (OECD) and the pure white IMBECILES they shepherd (predominantly but not exclusively pure white) that they are ULTRA-RIGHTEOUS GENIUSES, so they destroy ALL FOREIGNERS who know they are not. When Hereditary Racial Hatred unravels, it instantly mutates to CONSPIRACY THEORY.

OXFORD, ENGLAND: GDC, Pure White, Crooked, and Hereditary Racist Member of the Most Excellent Order of our own EMPIRE of Stolen Inheritance - **Habakkuk**, Mrs Helen Falcon (MBE), a ROTARIAN (vulgarly charitable, hereditary white supremacist, and Antichrist Freemasonry Quasi-Religion without voodoo or occultists' rituals), the archetypal member of the GDC Committee, the only official spouse of Mr Falcon, physically ill-favoured homunculus pure white bastard, with asymmetrical huge muscular ass like those of a professional javelin thrower (Fatima Whitbread), and the archetypal Postgraduate Dean, Oxford, unrelentingly lied under oath and on record

– **Habakkuk 1:4.** The poor pure white ancestors of her pure white father and mother were incompetent RACIST liars too, like the pure white ancestors of King's School and Oxbridge-educated Lord Justice Charles Anthony Haddon-Cave, KC, a RACIST son of a very, very, very, rich Tasmanian Colonialist Economic Cannibal (**Mark 10:25**), Sir Charles Phillip Haddon-Cave (1925-1999), and a closeted white supremacist descendant of DRUG LORDS (opium merchants of Qing Dynasty), an impostor and an expert of the deception (perception is always grander thanb reality), and a homie of Eton and Oxbridge-educated very, very, very, rich men's son, Archbishop Justin Welby (**Mark 10:25**), they were THIEVES and owners of stolen children of defenceless poor people, including the pure Black African ancestors of the IMPURE (<43% Nigerian) niece and nephew of the Prince of Wales.

A very, very, very, DISHONEST typical pure white Englishwoman. A crooked closeted hereditary RACIST Member of the Most Excellent Order of our Empire of Stolen Inheritance – **Habakkuk.**

"The English think incompetence is the same thing as sincerity." Quentin Crisp (1908-1999).

They don't want all their own mentally gentler white children (OECD) and all the pure white IMBECILES they shepherd (predominantly but not exclusively pure white) to know the TRUTH, which is that apart from our INFERIOR SKIN COLOUR, which we neither made nor chose, and our INFERIOR ACCENT of speaking a foreign language, we are not as bad as they truly feel, as we are also properly created by Almighty God, and to conceal this TRUTH, hereditary racist pure white bastards (predominantly but not exclusively pure white) criminally steal yields of our own people's (AFRICANS) Christ-granted talents, and their overwhelming RACIST LEVERAGE is the certainty that all Judges would be PURE WHITE, and their hope is that they would be hereditary white supremacist bastards too – **Habakkuk 1:4.**

They are not the only creation of Almighty God, and they are not immortal, and the universally acknowledged irrefutably SUPERIOR SKIN COLOUR that the very, very, very, fortunate wearer neither made nor chose is not the only wonder of our world.

Proverbs 20:15: Skin colour is a great creation of Almighty God, but it is not the greatest.

Based on several decades of very, very, very, proximate observations and direct experiences, they hate our own people, and we know, and they hate our own children more, but they don't know. They should stay here, it is safer. There, we will take revenge, but only LEGALLY, under God's Law – **Exodus 21:23-27.**

OYINBO OLE: A RACIST DESCENDANT OF ULTRA-RIGHTEOUS PURE WHITE THIEVES AND OWNERS OF STOLEN CHILDREN OF DEFENCELESS POOR PEOPLE – **HABAKKUK.**

Enduring Residues of the Original Sin (SLAVERY): Motivated by Hereditary Racial Hatred and Innate Envy, they brainlessly and baselessly self-awarded SUPREME KNOWLEDGE, and they maliciously impose the stereotypically Black African Learning Disability Education on Black African Children: The tyranny of the pure white majority.

Mark 10:25: Elon Musk: Hereditary Intra-Racial Sex Machine.

TWELVE: "Tyrannical Police State." Elon Musk.

Unlike her little brother, age saved the child's sister from the Closeted-Racist-Dylan–Roof-Freemason- Judge, Bedford's District Judge Paul Robert Ayers. She thanks her stars that the incontrovertibly functional semi-illiterate, closeted opportunist racist, and crooked pure white bastard, lowlife impostor and an expert of deception, did not have anything to do with her education.

In her GCSE, she gained the following grades:
English Language A*
English Literature A*
Mathematics A*
Additional Mathematics A*
Physics A*
Chemistry A*
Biology A*
History A*
Latin A
Spanish A
Advanced Level Mathematics A

Envy is a thief. Indiscreet envy.

"Envy is weak." Yul Brynner (1920-1985).

Only two years later, the pure Black sister of the pure Black Nigerian child, gained six A/Level grade As, and has since gained a First Class Master of Science Degree from one of the topmost universities in Great Britain.

OYINBO OLE/ODE: Shame and guilt. They don't want their own mentally gentler white children (OECD), and the pure white IMBECILES they shepherd (predominantly but not exclusively pure white) to know the TRUTH of MAAFA, which is that millions of stolen African children that their evil ancestors merciless killed, during several continuous centuries of very, very, very, perilous middle-passage (1445-1888), were also properly created by Almighty God.

The racist evil perilous middle passage when millions of stolen children of defenceless poor people were sadistically constructively unlawfully killed (**Exodus 20:13),** and became fish food.

RATZAK: Extremely nasty hands-off RACIST MURDERERS - **Exodus 20:13.**

Google: Dr Richard Bamgboye, GP. Google: Dr Anand Kamath, Dentist. They were unlawfully killed, albeit hands-off, with the hidden in the belly of the actus reus.

Based on several decades of very, very, very, proximate observations and direct experiences, they are like RATS, and like RATS, they love to act without being seen, and like RATS, they are excessively STUPID, as they defecate everywhere leaving tell-tale signs.

"There is no sin except stupidity." Wilde (1854-1900).

OYINBO OLE: Racist descendants of THIEVES (**Exodus 20:15**) and more familiar with direct descendants of PLANTATION NEGROES, such as Diane Abbott, Michelle Obama, Meghan Markle, Chris Eubanks, David Lammy Etcetera – who today bears the names of the owners of their direct ancestors, stolen African children who systematically genetically reversed, deliberately artificially paired up and bred for very, very, very, hard labour, and reared like cattle by very, very, very, highly civilised, and super-enlightened European Christians on Stolen Indian Land.

OYINBO OLE/ODE: The academic height that the pure white father and mother of District Judge Paul Robert Ayers CANNOT know, and which the natural talents of his own white children, grandchildren, and great grandchildren will not exploit.

"To deny or belittle this good is, in this dangerous century when the resources and pretensions of power continue to enlarge, a desperate error of intellectual abstraction. More than this, it is a self-fulfilling error, which encourages us to give up the struggle against bad laws and class bound procedures and to disarm ourselves before power. It is to throw away a whole inheritance of struggle about the law and within the forms of law, whose continuity can never be fractured without bringing men and women into immediate danger." - E. P Thompson (1923-1994).

"The white man is the devil." Brother Khalid Mohammed (1948-2001).

Based on several decades of very, very, very, proximate observations and direct experiences, the pure white man is the DEVIL.

Like Mark Fuhrman (LAPD), Bedford's District Judge Paul Robert Ayers, the Senior Vice President of the Association of Her Majesty District Judges is PURE WHITE, but Archie is impure, <43% Nigerian.

"I have seen evil, and it has the face of Mark Fuhrman." Johnny Cochran (1937-2005).

ABOUT THE AUTHOR:

The author was a boarder at Anglican Church Grammar School and at the University of Lagos.

Printed in Dunstable, United Kingdom